A Montana Table

Recipes from Chico Hot Springs Resort

A Montana Table

Recipes from Chico Hot Springs Resort

by Seabring Davis

photos by Carol Rublein

ThreeForks™

GUILFORD, CONNECTICUT
HELENA, MONTANA

AN IMPRINT OF THE GLOBE PEQUOT PRESS

ThreeForks is a trademark of The Globe Pequot Press.

Photo credits: All color and food photographs copyright Carol Rublein, Northern Exposure Photography. All black-and-white historical photographs courtesy of the Park County Museum.

Text design by GingerBee Creative.

Library of Congress Cataloging-in-Publication Data is available.

ISBN: 0-7627-2570-2

Manufactured in Great Britain
First Edition/First Printing

Contents

Preface

If someone had told me thirty years ago that I would become an innkeeper in Montana, (MONTANA?!) I would have told them they were completely off target, unrealistic, dreaming. Sometimes, though, other people's dreams become your own reality.

In my case, it was my husband, Mike, who had the dream and followed it by purchasing Chico Hot Springs (a run-down, sadly neglected little western hotel) without my ever having seen it! That was 1973. Mike's dream began as my nightmare. The place was a disaster! But I woke up from my nightmare and soon realized that Mike's foresight and vision would eventually become a lifestyle for our family that has provided us with endless bounty. We have been very lucky to have met so many wonderful people from all over the world who come to Chico as guests and leave as friends. We have the good fortune of having a dedicated, talented staff, which has become our extended family.

Over the years we learned by trial and error (and there were plenty of those!) that the hospitality business is an invaluable lesson in LIFE and really cannot be duplicated in a classroom setting. Our classroom setting is a spectacular 10,900-foot mountain with high peaks surrounding the resort on all sides—golden and rosy in the summer and capped by snow sprinkles in winter, and all this is graced by a natural hot spring that flows through the property. Not a bad place to go to work!

For us, gratitude is an ongoing process. For all the local folks who literally came to our rescue in the early, and often difficult days—Harold Marchington who fixed the tumbling barn roof (no pay); his wife, Margaret, who single-handedly cleaned the whole hotel (no pay for a long time); Elma Shimmins who came to help me cook for the guests when I begged her on my knees "please, Elma, just one more time"; Benna Busby who fried hamburgers in the old snack bar until past midnight if she had to; a local rancher who gave us the lovely barn wood you see in the Chico dining room today; and many others who gave so generously of themselves to make Chico into what it is today—a happy vacation getaway for our guests and a source of great pride for us. For all this grace and bounty we feel truly blessed and hope that as you try out the recipes in this book, you'll think fondly of us. And if you feel like it, share with us some of your thoughts. Now get cooking! —Eve Art

I can only add that this whole wonderful dream that has come true for me and my family could not have happened without the love, help, and support of my wife, Eve, my daughters, Andy and Jackie, and the literally hundreds of people who helped and still help run this "quirky" place. A special thank you to my friend and general manager, Colin Davis, who for the past six years has made "the cream rise to the top."

I, too, hope you will enjoy this book, use it, share it, and think of us with fond memories. I also hope you'll keep coming back to Chico and keep on keeping us on our toes. —Mike Art

Acknowledgments

This book would not have been possible without the Art family. Their hard work, wisdom, and determination is inspirational. I also owe this great opportunity to my husband, Colin Davis, who is Chico's general manager and managing partner. Many thanks to head chefs Chris Clark and Craig Flick, pastry chef Marlene Coogler, and the rest of the kitchen crew. Also, thank you to my editor, Megan Hiller, for her persistence, patience, and professionalism. And sincere thanks to recipe testers Sandi Igo, Melissa Pate, Cindy Bertsen, Kelly Kulbeck, Beth Renick, and Randi Jacobson. —Seabring Davis

Introduction

A Montana Icon

A visit to Chico Hot Springs can change your life. More than once we have come across people who moved to Montana simply because they discovered Chico. We know people who fell in love here, a woman who remembers twelve years of Sunday drives to Chico with her father for a swim, a man who has ordered the same meal in the dining room for the last fifteen years, and countless couples who have been married here.

This is a place built on nostalgia. People come here expecting to relive an experience from twenty years ago or to create a moment they will never forget. It is steeped in history, people, and food. This is not a glitzy spot. Chico is a Montana icon, full of good times and hard work. It is a place of simple roots located in a breathtaking valley with a constant flow of hot water. The hot water is the essence of Chico and we have never taken that for granted. It is a magical getaway that has changed with the times, yet at its core remains the same.

A long-time Chico patron said recently, Chico is an experience, and the food in the dining room represents that experience. It's true. If you only swim at Chico, you don't know it completely. If you only dance in the saloon, you haven't experienced it entirely. If you only go on a trail ride at Chico, you won't get the whole effect. Yet in the food you can savor each moment, engaging your senses completely to culminate your moment at Chico Hot Springs Resort. With these recipes we hope to share the spirit of Chico.

Making History

People began raving about the restaurant at Chico Hot Springs Resort more than 100 years ago. It started with a bowl of strawberries during the height of the Montana gold rush. Bill and Percie Knowles opened a modest boardinghouse near a natural hot springs. They catered to fortune-seeking miners who had grown weary of campfire meals, washing their clothes in the creek, and living a rugged way of life. What they offered was a clean bed, a hot bath, and fresh strawberries with every meal.

What the Knowles learned is that folks will travel far for a good soak and a fine meal. So, in 1900 the Knowles expanded their business and built Chico Warm Springs Hotel. Housed in a lovely clapboard building, boasting a full-service dining room, complete with white-linen tablecloths and fine china, as well as a 44-foot hot springs "plunge" pool, the 20-room inn was instantly popular. People came from all over the state to relish in the finery of Chico.

Back then the fare was simple, comfort food in a pleasant setting. The menu reflected the wholesome tastes of its clientele: meat and potatoes. The wine list consisted of three choices: red, white, and pink. But what made a meal at Chico most memorable were the fresh ingredients. Even in the chill of winter the restaurant used fresh produce—delicate lettuce, vine-ripened tomatoes, and of course, strawberries. Warm water from the hot spring fed into a large garden near the hotel, making it possible to harvest vegetables year-round. The Knowles knew then that using fresh, local ingredients was the key to a great meal.

News of the good food spread, as it always does.

A New Era

That was over a century ago and folks are still talking about the unforgettable dining at Chico Hot Springs. The clapboard hotel looks very much as it did when it first opened. Though today's restaurant services a broader clientele, the heart and soul of the menu is steeped in the simplicity of those early beginnings. With hearty seasonal preparations of beef, wild game, and seafood, the dining room at Chico has received unparalleled acclaim throughout the state and beyond. It wasn't always this way, however.

There was a time when Chico Hot Springs did not have a good reputation for food or cozy hotel rooms or anything else. After decades of neglect, the notable hotel fell into serious disrepair before it was resuscitated by Mike Art and his family in the 1970s. The hotel Mike and Eve Art walked into was in shambles. There was no clientele to speak of, and the business was flailing. Bit by bit, the Arts and their daughters, Andy and Jackie, began to rebuild the place. Alongside a few faithful employees, they did everything to make it work. They struggled to find reliable employees; both Mike and Eve pulled shifts in the kitchen to churn out family-style meals. The girls doubled as horse wranglers, housekeepers, and cooks/dishwashers between doing their homework.

In 1976, out of necessity and inspiration, the Arts decided to change the style of food at Chico to an upscale restaurant. Mike's idea was to create a destination dining experience. Eve's suggestion was to find a chef, not a cook. The result was a partnership with executive chef Larry Edwards. Plucked from a popular gathering place in Jackson Hole, Wyoming, Edwards brought an authentic passion for gourmet cuisine. Using influences from European fare and his discriminating palate, he transformed the menu for The Inn at Chico Hot Springs with rich, inventive culinary temptations that remain the model for Chico's food today. Signature dishes such as the Fennel Breadsticks, Artichoke with Curry Aioli, Duck L'Orange, and the Flaming Orange redefined dining in the region. Edwards's refined style and elegant food were new to Montana's dining scene—hungry or curious people came to taste it for themselves. Again the good news spread.

Business picked up, but the transition came slowly; many hands helped to make it happen. While Mike regularly drove as far as 200 miles or more to pick up fresh seafood or other necessary ingredients, Eve hosted in the dining room. Andy apprenticed with Edwards, learning the fine points of the food and beverage business, which led to her current, long-standing position as dining room manager. Jackie helped in her spare time as well, baking with her grandmother Irene. She perfected Chico's now famous New York Cheesecake.

By the late 1980s, Montana was a hot spot. Chico was known for its food and had a loyal following of local customers, but people from all over the country came to stay here. Melt in your mouth steaks, seafood, handmade mints, and flawless chocolate soufflés were special treats in the restaurant. On a busy night the dining room served 25 dinners. Later the numbers swelled to 90, and today the average is 180. Chico emerged as a fine dining destination and a success.

Food for Thought

Through the decades Chico has stayed true to its comfort food roots. Year by year a synthesis of culinary styles has improved upon Chico's beginnings. With Larry Edwards as the kitchen patriarch, other influential people have left their marks on Chico's menu: Blair Taylor, Marvin Garrett, Craig Flick, Matt Jackson, Joe Cobb, Chris Clark, Greg Coleman, Marlene Coogler, Kelly Keene, Justin Hewitt, Kelly Lehman, and Doug Wilson. Currently chefs Chris Clark and Craig Flick are at the culinary helm in the kitchen, carrying on the tradition of Chico. Like good stock for a soup, these talented people have been an essential base to Chico's cuisine.

These recipes are like heirlooms passed down to remind us that respite can come in something as elementary as a well-cooked meal. This food and its flavors are robust, laden with an earthy richness drawn from the hearty spirit of the West. Some of the recipes call for just a little time, while others call for the commitment of an entire day. In either case, the end result will be worthwhile.

Chico's kitchen still relies on fresh ingredients from the geothermal greenhouse and garden, as well as the local offerings of the area—Montana beef, farm-raised fowl, wild game, and regional trout. Signature dishes on the menu reflect the traditional hearty tastes: Rosemary Rack of Lamb, Beef Wellington, Pine Nut Crusted Halibut, and Smoked Trout. Yet there is also an element of refinement that has been integrated to bring out the sumptuousness of those basic foods. The result is a menu that is uniquely Montana—as appealing to a local rancher or a Hollywood celebrity as it is to the bon vivant.

This collection of recipes features Chico "classics," time-tested, long-standing favorites from the last twenty-five years of cooking at Chico Hot Springs Resort. The first half of the book is drawn directly from the menu in the dining room at Chico, while the entertaining section focuses on personalized menus for larger groups.

The first chapter, "Chico Mornings," features preparations from Chico's abundant Sunday brunch offerings. In "Starters," you'll find the secret ingredient for Fennel Breadsticks, along with the restaurant's best appetizers. Next, "From the Garden" walks you through the abundant homegrown vegetables essential in preparing salads, dressings, side dishes, and soups. Move into the heart of the matter with "Main Courses," followed by our decadent "Desserts."

Chico is a place that hosts many celebrations, from intimate family dinners to grand-scale weddings. In the "Entertaining Chico Style" chapter you'll find three select dinner menus and wine suggestions adapted for larger parties. Finally, "Chef's Cupboard" is a practical collection of basic recipes and resources.

Most of these recipes are written exactly the way they are prepared at Chico. Graciously, the kitchen crew meticulously broke down these dishes from massive quantities designed for commercial cooking to appropriate portions for home cooking. In consideration for the home chef, however, we have offered suggestions for substitutes when an ingredient is difficult to find or requires unusually extensive preparation. Today's specialty food markets offer high quality premade products that are exceptional substitutes.

Before you begin, decide which dish you would like to prepare, then gather the ingredients and the cooking equipment you will need. Remember, organization is key. Knowing the sequence of your recipe is the best way to relish each step that finally leads you to your own version of a Montana table.

Think of each meal you prepare as a piece of a story that began long ago on the frontier in Montana and continues today at Chico. Use these recipes wisely, because when the news of your good cooking spreads, you might have a lot of visitors as well.

Chico's History

Chico Warm Springs Hotel opened to the public on June 20, 1900, with a great celebration. Bill and Percie Knowles organized a delightful reception for their guests; news of the grand opening spread like wildfire through the area. Entertainment and dancing was provided for guests in an open-air

In the early 1900s, visitors came to Chico Hot Springs from near and far.

pavilion, located on the front lawn. A horse-drawn carriage shuttled guests the three miles to and from the Fridley railroad platform.

Back then the two-story clapboard hotel, showcased by its dormer windows and veranda extending along

The original hotel in autumn

the entire front of the building, was a charming sight set against a rugged landscape. The inn had accommodations for 40 guests and boasted a plunge 44 feet in diameter, six feet deep, and enclosed from the harsh weather. There were private baths and also baths for the ladies with a designated stairway entrance to the pool direct from the hotel.

It was a promising beginning for the new hotel. Business boomed, drawing travelers from

Chico employees pose with a child in 1909.

across the state. By the next year Bill Knowles expanded the hotel, adding 25 more rooms.

Proprietor Percie Knowles had a long-term vision for Chico to become a health spa. After her husband died, she shut down the saloon and stopped serving alcohol. In June of 1912 she procured the reputable services of a Doctor George A. Townsend, whose later successful treatment of patients with ailments such as the common cold to conditions requiring brain surgery gained considerable recognition as far as North Dakota, Minnesota, and eastern states as well. Chico's mineral pools were touted as a curative for kidney disease and other ailments. The doctor's

Three beautiful bathers enjoy the warm water on July 4, 1912.

success was a huge draw for guests and with that came many additions to the property.

By 1916 a 20-room hospital wing was built onto the hotel. The new building accommodated 24 patients and included a lab, operating room, and six examination rooms. Dr. Townsend practiced here until 1925, when he finally retired and moved to Glacier Park.

During the Great Depression Chico hit hard times. A brochure produced in 1939 advertised room rates for $2.75 per day or $17 a week, including breakfast and dinner, as well as use of all bathing

Some of the waitresses and housekeepers
in their uniforms, 1915

and plunge privileges. Cabins rented for $1 daily or $20 a month per person. The public could swim in the hot springs for 25 cents. Another brochure from 1946 featuring the same photos listed higher room prices at $4 per day or $24 per week and cabins for $1.50 a day or $30 per month.

High times at Chico dwindled after Percie's death. Her son sold the hotel and Chico experienced many changes at the hands of various owners. It went from health resort to dude ranch to religious retreat to roadhouse and eventually into complete disrepair.

Finally when Mike and Eve Art purchased the dilapidated property in 1973, the hotel was falling apart, the famous pool was slimy with algae, and

*Surgery was performed
at Chico's very successful hospital
by Dr. Townsend in the mid-1900s.*

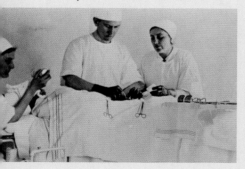

there were only a few intermittent guests. The plumbing in the main lodge was ancient, the heat was faulty, and the rooms were described at best as "funky." The

Arts began their ownership that winter with only three loyal employees and their two young daughters. Everybody had their share of work, whether it was cleaning bathrooms, cooking the family-style meals, or working the front desk. The early years of their new venture were full of lessons, hard work, and new experiences. In retrospect, the growing pains they experienced as innkeepers seem humorous to the

Arts, but in the moment, the family struggled to bring the tumbled resort back to life.

Incrementally the family made improvements on the place. At first simple things, such as repairing the heating system and fixing leaks in the roof. Then the changes became more prominent, chiefly the addition of the restaurant that changed the way people thought of Chico.

Chico Dining Room, 1939

Over two decades Chico progressed as the Arts increased the number of lodging possibilities with cabins and hotel rooms. Through the 1980s and 1990s, Montana became a popular destination and the Arts adapted to their clientele by building an elegant convention center and restoring a historic

Eve and Mike Art

portion of the main lodge—the Warren Wing, adding 20 modern rooms. The Arts have been careful and conscientious in making improvements that are true to the property's historic past. The allure of Chico Hot Springs Resort is that at its core it is still the same quaint and simple retreat that was built more than a century ago, but now offers all the modern amenities of today.

Caramel Rolls ▶

Chico Mornings

Caramel Rolls

(see photo page 1)

After an arduous week working on a travel story about Chico Hot Springs, the editorial staff from Outdoor Life *magazine returned to New York City. Within 48 hours after arriving home the crew bemoaned their life without Chico's Caramel Rolls. Chico promptly sent two dozen rolls overnight. This recipe is that good.*

dough:
　　2½ cups, plus 2 tablespoons all-purpose flour
　　6 tablespoons sugar
　　1 tablespoon instant yeast
　　½ teaspoon cinnamon
　　¾ teaspoon salt
　　¾ cup water
　　1½ tablespoons unsalted butter
　　2 tablespoons, plus ¼ teaspoon vegetable shortening
　　1 egg

filling:
　　½ pound (2 sticks) unsalted butter, softened
　　1 cup firmly packed brown sugar
　　1½ teaspoons cinnamon

topping:
　　1 cup heavy whipping cream
　　1 cup firmly packed brown sugar

To prepare dough: Combine flour, sugar, yeast, cinnamon, and salt in the bowl of an electric mixer, or in a large mixing bowl if preparing by hand. In a saucepan heat water, butter, and shortening until it reaches about 120° to 130°. Break egg into a medium bowl. Slowly pour the butter mixture into the egg while whisking. Add this mixture to the dry ingredients in your mixing bowl fitted with a dough hook or use a large metal spoon to mix, adding additional flour to make a soft workable dough. Place in a greased bowl and cover with plastic wrap. Let the dough rise until doubled in size (about 30 to 45 minutes).

To prepare filling: While dough is rising, mix the butter, brown sugar, and cinnamon until it reaches a paste consistency. Set aside.

To prepare topping: Combine cream and brown sugar and whip until they reach a sour

cream–like consistency. Cover the bottom of a 9 x 13-inch glass baking dish with topping, and set aside.

Preheat oven to 350°. When dough is ready, roll into an 18 x 10-inch rectangle about ⅛ inch thick. Spread the filling on the dough and roll tightly lengthwise. Cut into 1-inch-thick rolls and place on topping in glass dish. Rolls should be almost touching. Cover the pan with plastic wrap and let rise once more until almost doubled, about 30 minutes. Remove the plastic and bake for 30 minutes, or until topping is golden and clear.

Remove pan from oven and immediately remove rolls by inverting pan onto a serving tray or baking sheet. Pour any excess liquid over the rolls. Let cool slightly and serve.

Yields 1 dozen

It Can Happen at Chico

Food isn't the only thing happening at Chico Hot Springs Resort. This is a place for celebrating, conducting business, and gathering with the ones you love. From family reunions to annual meetings, Chico offers the perfect venue for any occasion.

Whether you are throwing a birthday bash or a formal wedding, the Convention Center on the main lawn can fill your needs. Constructed in 1998 with classic stone and white clapboard, the building maintains a historic quality to match the vintage hotel. It has all the charm of old Chico with modern amenities, including a fully equipped banquet kitchen and bar.

Encircled by windows, a large stone fireplace accents the majestic room, which can comfortably seat 250 guests. The space can also be scaled down for smaller groups; it converts into three separate rooms and creates a more intimate space.

Each year many organizations return to Chico to conduct business. It's an ideal setting to get away from the everyday fray of the office and be productive. For smaller meetings or retreats, the sophisticated board room in the Lower Lodge or the cozy wine room easily seat 16 to 20 people. With a large assortment of activities and dining facilities on the property, your guests will never need to leave; everything you desire is out the front door. At Chico you can relax, think, work, and then play a little.

In the early days (circa 1920), Chico's Saloon was known as a place for the boys to hang out.

Sour Cream Coffee Cake

Delicate and dense, this cake is just as satisfying for dessert as it is for breakfast. Berries work best with this recipe, but other fruits such as peaches, or even cherries, are lovely, too.

8 tablespoons (1 stick) unsalted butter, softened and cubed
1 cup granulated sugar
3 eggs
2 cups all-purpose flour
2 teaspoons baking powder
1 teaspoon baking soda
2 cups sour cream
1½ teaspoons pure vanilla extract
1 pint fresh blueberries (or fruit of your choice; frozen fruit can be substituted)
¼ cup powdered sugar for dusting

Preheat oven to 350°. Spray a 9-inch springform pan with cooking spray. Cream butter and sugar in a mixing bowl. Add eggs one at a time, scraping sides and bottom of bowl between additions. Sift flour, baking powder, and baking soda together. Alternately add dry ingredients and sour cream to butter mixture. Add vanilla and combine thoroughly, but do not overmix.

Spread half the batter in the prepared springform pan. Place a layer of fruit on top of the batter. Carefully spread remaining batter on top of the fruit, using a metal spatula dipped in hot water to evenly distribute the batter to the edges of the pan. Bake for 30 to 45 minutes, or until the cake is firm to the touch; a toothpick inserted should come out clean. Cool completely and remove from pan. Sprinkle with powdered sugar and garnish with remaining fruit.

Serves 8

Granola

With milk or yogurt, this house-made granola gives you a hearty start to the day. Made with walnuts, almonds, coconut, and sunflower seeds, this cereal has a healthy dose of protein wrapped up in a sweet maple-honey flavor. Serve it with warm milk on cold winter days for a great alternative to oatmeal.

3 cups rolled oats
1¼ cups bran flakes
¾ cup shredded sweetened coconut
½ cup chopped walnuts
1 cup sliced almonds
¾ cup salted sunflower seeds
2 teaspoons cinnamon
2½ teaspoons pure maple syrup
¾ cup honey
¾ cup canola oil

Preheat oven to 350°. Prepare two baking sheets by covering with wax or parchment paper and grease paper with cooking spray. Combine oats, bran flakes, coconut, walnuts, almonds, sunflower seeds, and cinnamon in a large bowl. In a separate bowl, mix maple syrup, honey, and oil; add to dry mixture and stir until well combined. Divide the mixture between each prepared cookie sheet; spread evenly. Bake for 20 to 25 minutes until golden brown, tossing granola halfway through baking time to keep edges from burning. Let cool completely before storing.

Yields ½ gallon

French Toast

Thick, hearty bread is essential for this breakfast staple. The corn flakes create a pleasing crunchy crust to accompany the fluffy center.

1 cup heavy whipping cream
5 eggs
1 teaspoon cinnamon
1 teaspoon nutmeg
2 teaspoons pure vanilla extract
1 cup corn flakes
1 loaf Heirloom Bread, sliced (recipe page 19), or 8 slices whole wheat bread
Corn or canola oil to coat bottom of the skillet

toppings:
Powdered sugar
Pure maple syrup
Fresh berries

Chill a large mixing bowl for batter. Combine cream, eggs, cinnamon, nutmeg, and vanilla; mix thoroughly. Set corn flakes on a plate or in a shallow bowl.

Heat large skillet with canola or corn oil on medium-high heat. Dip both sides of bread slices in batter, then coat with corn flakes. Add slices to heated skillet quickly before bread gets soggy. Cook each side until golden brown. Sprinkle with powdered sugar; serve with pure maple syrup and fresh berries.

Serves 4

Montana Snowball Cookies

Brunch at Chico is an extensive meal; dessert is included in the big splurge. Tuck a couple of these sweet treats into your pocket to sneak while you are out dog sledding. It'll take the chill out of the real snow and give you a quick burst of energy so you can keep up with the dogs.

½ pound (2 sticks) unsalted butter
½ cup sifted powdered sugar
1 teaspoon pure vanilla extract
2¼ cups all-purpose flour
¼ teaspoon salt
¼ cup finely chopped pecans
½ cup powdered sugar for dusting

Preheat oven to 400°. Cream butter and sugar until light and fluffy. Add vanilla, flour, salt and pecans; mix until a loose dough ball forms. Roll into 1-inch balls and place on a baking sheet about two inches apart. Bake for 10 to 12 minutes. Remove from oven and immediately roll hot cookies in powdered sugar to coat. Let cookies cool and roll in powdered sugar again.

Yields 3 dozen cookies

Eggplant Timbale

This tasty dish is a tempting alternative to quiche and considerably easier than a soufflé. The eggs and the sour cream combine to give it a light, creamy texture. It's perfect as a side dish or a special item for an afternoon brunch.

1 red bell pepper
4 eggs, beaten
¼ cup sour cream
½ cup shredded Monterey Jack cheese
½ cup bread crumbs
2 tablespoons chopped fresh parsley, divided
1 medium yellow onion, diced
2 shallots, diced
2 tablespoons unsalted butter
2 medium eggplants

Roast bell pepper over an open flame on a gas-burning stovetop or grill; remove from flame when skin is mostly blackened and immerse pepper in an ice bath to remove skin easily. Seed and dice. Pepper can also be roasted in a 400-degree oven for 10 to 20 minutes.

In a bowl, mix half of the red bell pepper, beaten eggs, sour cream, cheese, bread crumbs and 1 tablespoon parsley. Sauté onion and shallots in butter until sweated. Add to bowl.

Slice eggplant in ¼-inch rounds, keeping the skin on and discarding the end pieces. Grill or sauté the eggplant until soft but not mushy.

Preheat oven to 350°. Line the bottom and sides of a well-greased 8-inch custard bowl or terrine mold with slices of cooked eggplant. Be sure to cover all surface area by overlapping eggplant slices; you will have leftover eggplant slices. Then place the mixed ingredients into the eggplant bowl. Top with the remaining eggplant.

Place the eggplant bowl in a separate baking dish filled with hot water; the water should come halfway up the outside of the bowl. Bake for 25 minutes. Press gently on the top of the eggplant to check for readiness; it should feel firm.

Remove from the oven and let stand in the water bath for 10 minutes. To serve, run a knife around the sides of dish to release the eggplant. Put a large serving plate on top of timbale and flip it over. Lift the bowl; the timbale should come out easily. Tap the bottom of the bowl if it sticks. Sprinkle the remaining red pepper and parsley on top for garnish.

Serves 8

Bacon, Leek, and Sundried Tomato Quiche

The quiche selection varies each Sunday at Chico's brunch; this is one of the favorites.

crust:
2 tablespoons unsalted butter
2 tablespoons shortening
1 cup all-purpose flour
¼ cup milk

batter:
6 eggs
1 cup heavy whipping cream
½ teaspoon black pepper
½ teaspoon dried mustard

filling:
1½ cups chopped, uncooked bacon
½ cup chopped sundried tomatoes
1 medium leek, cleaned and sliced
½ cup grated Cheddar cheese
½ cup grated Monterey Jack cheese

To prepare crust: Preheat oven to 350°. Grease an 8-inch pie pan with cooking spray. Combine butter, shortening, and flour. Blend ingredients with a fork until butter and shortening are fully incorporated; the dough will be slightly lumpy. Add milk and mix until ingredients are just wet. Roll out dough and press into prepared pie pan. Bake for 7 minutes; set aside.

To prepare batter: Mix all ingredients in a bowl and set aside.

To prepare filling and assemble quiche: Brown bacon and drain the excess grease, leaving the bacon in the pan. Add sundried tomatoes and leeks to the hot pan and return to heat. Cook until leeks become translucent.

Reduce oven temperature to 300°. Line the bottom of the reserved crust with Monterey Jack cheese. Cover with bacon, tomato, and leek mixture; top with Cheddar cheese; and pour egg batter for top layer. Place on a baking sheet to catch overflow during baking. Bake for 30 to 40 minutes, or until quiche is golden brown and firm.

Serves 8

Cinnamon Bread Pudding
with Vanilla Bourbon Sauce ▶

Cinnamon Bread Pudding
with Vanilla Bourbon Sauce

(see photo page 11)

This is a true comfort-food dessert. Baking it will fill your house with the warm, welcoming aromas of brown sugar, cinnamon, and vanilla. You can use any kind of bread or pastry—stale French bread, doughnuts, cinnamon rolls, cake crumbs. But consider the occasion, because it will be a more refined dish if you use the same kind of bread for the whole dish.

Cinnamon Bread Pudding:
    1 cup firmly packed brown sugar
    10 cups chopped day-old bread or pastry
    3 cups half-and-half
    2 cups heavy whipping cream
    ½ cup sugar
    5 eggs
    1 tablespoon cinnamon

Vanilla Bourbon Sauce:
    4 cups heavy whipping cream
    2 cups firmly packed brown sugar
    1 tablespoon pure vanilla extract
    ¼ teaspoon cinnamon
    ¼ to ½ cup bourbon (can also substitute brandy or orange liqueur)
    1 tablespoon cornstarch (optional)

To prepare Cinnamon Bread Pudding: Mix all ingredients in a large bowl; let soak for 20 minutes, stirring occasionally.

Preheat oven to 350°. Spray a 9 x 13-inch baking dish with cooking spray. Spray a piece of aluminum foil to use for covering later. Pour bread pudding batter into pan. Cover with foil and bake for one hour, or until center of pudding is firm. (Can be made one or two days in advance; reheat at 250° for about 30 minutes before serving.)

To prepare Vanilla Bourbon Sauce: Pour heavy cream into a saucepan and bring to a gentle boil on medium heat. Continue to boil until cream is reduced by almost half (about 30 minutes). Be careful to stir periodically to keep cream from scalding. Add brown sugar, vanilla, cinnamon, and bourbon, and allow to boil until sauce thickens

slightly (another 15 minutes). For extra thick sauce, add a tablespoon of cornstarch to the boiling liquid, stirring constantly.

Serve warm, drizzling sauce over the top of each pudding square after placing on a plate.

Serves 12

Citrus Salmon

Delicious and simple, the tangy marinade in this recipe offers a perfect balance for salmon's oily flesh. On any given Sunday you will find this dish offered at Chico's extensive brunch buffet. It is also wonderful for dinner.

Zest and juice of 2 oranges
½ cup chopped fresh parsley
2 tablespoons chopped garlic
Juice of 1 lime
1 cup extra virgin olive oil
6 (6-ounce) boneless salmon steaks

Preheat oven to 400°. Grease a roasting pan or baking dish (at least 9 x 13 inches) with cooking spray. In a bowl, combine orange zest, parsley, garlic, lime juice, and olive oil. Arrange salmon in the prepared pan or dish. Liberally brush on citrus–parsley mixture; let stand 10 minutes.

Pour orange juice over the top of fish and bake for 10 minutes. Salmon should be tender and flaky when finished.

Serves 6

Four-Cheese Quiche

Sunday brunch at Chico is a weekend tradition. Begin the meal with a refreshing mimosa and then indulge in the lavish buffet. Quiches, Citrus Salmon, thick and crispy bacon, cheesecakes, Cinnamon Bread Pudding, half a dozen different pastries, and an omelet bar are just a few of the items offered.

crust:
    2 tablespoons unsalted butter
    2 tablespoons shortening
    1 cup all-purpose flour
    ¼ cup milk

batter:
    6 eggs
    1 cup heavy whipping cream
    ½ teaspoon black pepper
    ½ teaspoon dried mustard

filling:
    ½ cup shredded medium-sharp Cheddar cheese
    ½ cup shredded Monterey Jack cheese
    ½ cup shredded Swiss cheese
    ½ cup shredded smoked Gouda cheese

To prepare crust: Preheat oven to 350°. Grease an 8-inch pie pan with cooking spray. Combine butter, shortening, and flour. Blend ingredients with a fork until butter and shortening are fully incorporated; the dough will be slightly lumpy. Add milk and mix until ingredients are just wet. Roll out dough and press into prepared pan. Bake for 7 minutes. Set aside. Reduce oven temperature to 300°.

To prepare batter: Mix all ingredients in a bowl and set aside.

To prepare filling and assemble quiche: Combine all cheeses. In the reserved pie crust, add all cheeses and pour egg batter over the top. Place on a baking sheet to catch overflow during baking. Bake for 30 to 40 minutes, or until quiche is golden brown and firm.

Serves 8

Fennel Breadsticks ▶

Starters

Fennel Breadsticks

(see photo page 17)

In the last twenty-five years that Chico has served these breadsticks with dinner, our guests have requested this recipe most. They are light and crisp, not doughy; the secret is not to overknead or overmix and to roll them out thinly before baking.

½ cup warm beer
½ cup warm water (approximately 110°)
1½ teaspoons instant yeast
3 cups bread flour (a high-gluten flour)
¾ teaspoon salt
½ cup extra virgin olive oil
3 tablespoons fennel seeds
1 egg
¼ cup heavy whipping cream

Mix beer, warm water, and yeast; let sit until it bubbles, about 10 minutes. Add flour, salt, olive oil, and fennel seeds, then combine in the bowl of an electric mixer fitted with a dough hook attachment or knead by hand until smooth. Do not overmix. If dough is sticky, add more flour. Place in a well-oiled bowl and let dough rise in a warm place until it doubles in size, about one hour.

Preheat oven to 425°. Prepare a baking sheet by covering it with wax or parchment paper, then grease with cooking spray. Flatten dough to about 1-inch thick with a rolling pin, then cut into 8-inch-long, 1-inch-wide strips. Roll the strips by hand into long, rounded breadsticks; cut in half. Place sticks on baking sheet.

Whisk egg and heavy whipping cream together; use a brush to coat breadsticks with egg wash. Bake for 15 to 20 minutes, or until golden brown.

Yields 4 dozen

Heirloom Bread

This simple French bread recipe is baked daily in the Chico kitchen and served at every table in the dining room. In the restaurant we prepare it in the baguette form—long and thin—for uniformity. But at home you can be more creative, try braiding one loaf or twisting another to give this staple a decorative flair.

    8 cups bread flour (a high-gluten flour)
    1 tablespoon salt
    3 cups warm water (approximately 110°)
    2 teaspoons instant yeast
    ½ cup cornmeal
    1 egg white
    ½ teaspoon salt

Place flour, salt, water, and yeast into an electric mixer fitted with a dough hook. If you are mixing the bread by hand, be sure to use swift, strong strokes to prevent overmixing. Combine ingredients thoroughly, adding more flour as necessary to achieve a soft smooth texture. Knead for 10 minutes.

Move dough to a clean bowl (do not coat in oil) and cover with plastic wrap. Let rise until it doubles in size (about 1 to 1½ hours). Gently punch down dough and divide into two equal pieces. Let rest five minutes. Flatten each piece into an oval and form into desired shape. Be careful not to knead or handle it too much at this stage, because it will become tough. Place on baking sheet sprinkled with corn meal or into a French loaf bread pan. Cover and let rise until the loaves almost double in size (about 30 minutes).

Preheat oven to 425°. Combine the egg white and salt; brush loaves generously with the mixture. Slash loaves diagonally with a sharp serrated knife in three or four places. Bake for 15 minutes, and then reduce heat to 375°. Bake 30 minutes more until bread is golden and crusty.

Yields 2 loaves

Artichokes with Curry Aioli

During dinner service, each table is served a small plate of chilled artichokes with this curry mayonnaise. It's a simple extra, but a memorable one. The recipe is also simple, though delicious.

    4 large artichokes

Curry Aioli:
    1 cup mayonnaise
    1 tablespoon yellow curry (mild)

To prepare artichokes: Cut stems if desired. (The stems taste as good as the heart, so you can also leave them.) Trim the thorny tips of the outside leaves with scissors, and with a serrated knife slice off the top. Place artichokes in a steaming basket over 1 to 2 inches of boiling water. Cook covered until tender, about 25 to 35 minutes for medium artichokes and up to 45 minutes for large artichokes. Test for tender readiness by plucking a leaf from the middle of the vegetable; if it pulls out easily, artichokes are done. Refrigerate until chilled.

To prepare Curry Aioli: Combine mayonnaise and curry, and stir until thoroughly combined.

Before serving, cut chilled artichokes in quarters and scoop out the fuzzy portion at the center of the artichoke, but be sure not to cut any of the treasured heart, the best part. Lay sliced-side down on a plate. Spoon the Curry Aioli into a small side dish or ramekin for dipping and serve.

Serves 4

Mushroom Pepper Sauté

This appetizer is served tableside sizzling in a 6-inch cast iron skillet, which is best for retaining heat. In the kitchen the dish is prepared over extremely high heat to sear and seal the flavors of garlic and butter into the vegetables. Ideally, you will want to serve this right out of the skillet, but if that is not possible it's acceptable to serve in an oven-warmed platter or bowl. It can also be served as a side dish with your main course.

4 tablespoons (½ stick) unsalted butter
32 brown mushrooms
1½ cups white wine
6 tablespoons minced garlic
1 red bell pepper, chopped
1 yellow bell pepper, chopped
1 green bell pepper, chopped
Salt and pepper to taste

Heat cast iron skillet on high heat for one minute. Add butter and mushrooms. Add white wine when the mushrooms are brown and stir gently; add garlic and peppers; salt and pepper to taste. Cook for two minutes. Serve in an oven-warmed bowl or platter.

Serves 4

Smoked Trout

The cooks at Chico take fresh farm-raised trout and marinate it in curry, salt, and brown sugar, then smoke it over alder wood until it reaches a firm, flaky perfection. The process takes two days and is well worth the effort. For home preparation, you should purchase smoked trout or substitute smoked salmon.

Toasted Almond and Dill Cream Cheese:
Zest and juice of ½ lemon
2 tablespoons sliced toasted almonds
¼ cup sour cream
8 ounces cream cheese, room temperature
1 teaspoon minced fresh dill
½ teaspoon salt

Tomato-Caper Relish:
3 large Roma tomatoes, seeds removed, diced
1 small red onion, diced
¼ cup capers
¼ cup chopped fresh chives
2 tablespoons cider vinegar
2 tablespoons minced fresh parsley
Salt and pepper to taste

4 to 5 ounces of boneless smoked trout
1 loaf French bread or Chico Heirloom Bread (recipe page 19)

To prepare Toasted Almond and Dill Cream Cheese: Thoroughly combine all ingredients together until easy to spread.

To prepare Tomato-Caper Relish: Mix all ingredients together.

Display the trout in one piece on a platter, with the cream cheese spread and the relish on the side with sliced fresh bread.

Serves 4

Oysters Rockefeller

Chico started serving this timeless hors d'oeuvre in 1976. It was a kind of delicacy in Montana at the time, since fresh seafood was not readily available. Fresh oysters were flown in once a week to Billings (about 200 miles away), and the owners would go pick up the order. Today, with fresh seafood flown into Bozeman daily and delivered to Chico, it's easier to offer oysters on the menu.

2 dozen raw oysters on the half shell
2 slices bacon, julienned
1 large yellow onion, diced
2 tablespoons minced garlic
2 cups fresh spinach, julienned
1 tablespoon anisette liqueur
¾ cup heavy whipping cream
¼ cup grated Parmesan cheese
¾ cup Hollandaise Sauce (recipe page 113)
2 cups coarse salt

Preheat oven to 450°. Render julienned bacon in large sauté pan. Add onion, cook until translucent. Combine garlic, spinach, anisette, and cream; mix with bacon and onion. Cook until spinach is wilted. Remove from heat. Spoon one heaping teaspoon of spinach mixture onto each oyster and sprinkle with Parmesan. Top each oyster with a dollop of Hollandaise Sauce, about ½ teaspoon. Serve oysters nestled in a bed of coarse salt.

Serves 4

Garden Oyster

Baked like Oysters Rockefeller, but with fresh tomatoes and herbs, this is a light summer appetizer. At Chico our chefs use house-smoked tomatoes, although here the ingredients call for regular Romas. Add a little extra Tabasco, replace the Monterey Jack cheese with Parmesan or Swiss—this is a flexible recipe and calls for whatever suits your taste.

2 dozen raw oysters on the half shell
Tabasco sauce
2 Roma tomatoes, sliced into rings
2 tablespoons chopped fresh parsley
2 tablespoons chopped fresh chives
Salt and pepper to taste
1 lemon
1 cup grated Monterey Jack cheese
Paprika

Preheat oven to 450°. Splash a couple dashes of Tabasco on top of each oyster, then top with a slice of tomato. Sprinkle parsley and chives, salt and pepper to taste. Cut the lemon into quarters and squeeze over the oysters, top with cheese. Sprinkle with paprika for extra color. Bake for 10 minutes, until cheese melts and begins to bubble.

Serves 4

Baked Brie with Huckleberry Coulis and Hollandaise Sauce

There are about forty species of huckleberries, all native to North America. In Montana the black huckleberry, dark purple in color, is the most widespread. Huckleberries are difficult to come by, even in Montana; appropriate substitutes in this dish are lingonberry, currant, or blackberry preserves. Regardless of which fruit you choose, what is essential for this starter is that the berry sauce balances the creamy Hollandaise with a precise sweetness and tartness. Timing is also key with this dish; the baked Brie and sauces should be served immediately.

1 loaf of French bread or Chico Heirloom Bread (recipe page 19)

Baked Brie:
  8 ounces Brie
  4 (5 x 5-inch) puffed pastry shells (available at most grocery stores in the frozen dessert section)
  3 eggs
  ¼ cup half-and-half

Huckleberry Coulis:
  1 cup huckleberry preserves
  Zest of 1 orange
  ½ cup cranberry juice

1 cup Hollandaise Sauce (recipe page 113)

Cut bread diagonally into 1-inch slices, save for later.

To prepare Baked Brie: Preheat oven to 450°. Trim the rind of the Brie so that only the soft, creamy portion remains. Cut cheese into 4 (2-ounce) squares. Gently wrap the pastry around the cheese as if you are wrapping a present; with your fingers crease the folds of the pastry to secure the dough until smooth.

Beat the eggs and half-and-half until mixed thoroughly for an egg wash (this will prevent the pastry from burning in the oven). Dip each pastry-wrapped Brie in the egg wash and place on a parchment-lined baking sheet. Bake until golden brown, about 15 to 20 minutes. The cheese should be melted in center of pastry. Check for doneness by inserting a toothpick into the center of the puff pastry; if the toothpick comes out clean, Brie is done.

To prepare Huckleberry Coulis: Place all ingredients into a blender or food processor, puree until smooth. Set aside.

To serve: Pour the Hollandaise Sauce onto an oversized platter or four individual serving plates, covering the surfaces completely. Next, drizzle Huckleberry Coulis in parallel lines to create decorative stripes over the Hollandaise Sauce. Place baked Brie squares on top of sauce. Serve the sliced bread in another dish or around the edge of the serving dish.

Serves 4

Tomato-Basil Bruschetta

Using fresh basil and tomatoes from the Chico garden or greenhouse, this appetizer is a favorite throughout the year. The three different sauces used in the recipe add layers of fresh flavor, putting a new spin on this classic Italian dish.

Tomato and Basil Salsa:

    15 Roma tomatoes, seeds removed, and diced
    3 tablespoons extra virgin olive oil
    3 tablespoons balsamic vinegar
    2 tablespoons minced garlic
    ½ tablespoon salt
    4 tablespoons julienned fresh basil

Goat Cheese Spread:

    2 ounces goat cheese
    4 tablespoons (½ stick) unsalted butter
    ½ teaspoon powdered mustard
    1 teaspoon Worcestershire sauce
    ¼ teaspoon granulated onion
    1 teaspoon chopped fresh chives

    2 loaves French bread
    ½ cup grated Parmesan cheese
    ½ cup Balsamic Vinegar Reduction Sauce (recipe page 110)
    ½ cup Basil Oil (recipe page 110)

To prepare Tomato and Basil Salsa: Preheat oven to 400°. Mix tomatoes, olive oil, vinegar, garlic, and salt together. Spread the mixture evenly on a baking sheet and roast in the oven for 8 to 10 minutes. Remove the tomatoes and let cool. Once cool, add basil and toss.

To make Goat Cheese Spread: Mix all ingredients together until smooth.

Preheat oven to 450°. Cut bread at an angle into 1-inch-thick slices. Generously spread Goat Cheese Spread on each slice and place on a baking sheet. Sprinkle with some of the Parmesan cheese and bake until golden brown (about 5 minutes). While bread is still hot, top with Tomato-Basil Salsa and sprinkle with remaining Parmesan cheese. Drizzle Balsamic Vinegar Reduction Sauce and Basil Oil alternately over bruschetta and serve.

Serves 4 to 6

Classic Escargot

Chico has been dishing this up since the 1970s and it is a consummate favorite.
The trick to this savory French classic is to serve it sizzling hot.

24 medium brown mushrooms, stems removed
1 tablespoon canola oil
1 cup white wine
24 large Helix snails
6 ounces Garlic Butter (recipe page 112)
4 ounces prosciutto, julienned
Salt and pepper to taste

Preheat oven to 450°. Sauté all mushroom caps in canola oil until brown. Add white wine, cook for two minutes, and remove from heat. Place mushrooms caps down in a casserole dish or oven-safe platter. Place a snail inside each mushroom, top with Garlic Butter and prosciutto. Bake for 6 to 8 minutes until butter is boiling. Serve immediately with butter still bubbling.

Serves 4

Classic Spinach Salad ▶

Naming Chico

The geothermal pools at the base of the Absaroka Mountains were used for centuries by Native American tribes who called this region home—the Crow, Flathead, Sioux, and Sheepeaters. It wasn't until the height of Montana's gold rush when miners seeking their fortunes settled at nearby Emigrant Gulch and put the place on the map. In fact, the first written record of the springs was found scrawled in the diary of a miner named John S. Hackney.

Vintage Chico Hot Springs sign from the 1950s

"I went out to the hot springs and washed my dirty duds," he wrote on January 16, 1865.

Even the name "Chico" was inspired by a man who visited the mining camp in 1866. Though this tale has never been historically verified, the story goes that a Hispanic worker accompanied an exploration party traveling through what would later become Yellowstone National Park. He entertained the Emigrant Gulch miners by the campfire with stories of spewing geysers and bubbling mud. He made such an impression on the settlement that when the encampment was relocated in 1868 the miners dubbed the hot springs Chico in their new friend's honor.

From the Garden

Classic Spinach Salad

(see photo page 31)

This recipe appeared in the 1988 issue of Bon Appetit *and is Chico's signature salad. Grown in the garden behind the restaurant, fresh spinach is coated with this creamy dressing to give it a rich flavor.*

Creamy Italian Dressing:

    1 cup mayonnaise
    2 tablespoons Italian herb seasoning
    2 tablespoons granulated garlic
    1 teaspoon sugar
    1 tablespoon extra virgin olive oil
    2 tablespoons red wine vinegar
    1½ cups half-and-half

    1 pound spinach
    1 small red onion, thinly sliced
    ½ cup bacon, browned and chopped
    2 eggs, hard boiled and chopped

To prepare Creamy Italian Dressing: Blend mayonnaise, Italian seasoning, garlic, and sugar in a blender. With machine running, slowly drizzle in olive oil and then vinegar. Gradually add half-and-half and blend until smooth. Chill until needed.

To prepare salad: Toss dressing with spinach and onion until leaves are coated. Divide between plates and top with bacon and eggs.

Serves 4

Thai Duck Salad

The succulent duck adds a touch of elegance and richness to this simple salad. It is ideal for a light meal as well as for a dinner salad. Prepare the Thai Vinaigrette a day in advance of serving it on this salad.

Thai Vinaigrette:

   Juice of 1 lime
   1 tablespoon minced garlic
   1 tablespoon brown sugar
   2 cups rice wine vinegar
   ¾ cup extra virgin olive oil
   2 teaspoons sesame oil
   1 tablespoon honey
   2 tablespoons Tabasco sauce

   1 roasted Muscovy duck
   1 pound mixed greens
   1 red pepper, sliced
   5 scallions, chopped
   ¼ cup canned mandarin orange segments, drained

To prepare Thai Vinaigrette: Mix all ingredients together and let stand overnight.

Remove skin from cooled duck and shred meat by hand; place in a large bowl. In a separate bowl, combine mixed greens, red pepper, and scallions; add duck meat. Just before serving, add mandarin oranges and toss salad with Thai Vinaigrette, coating thoroughly.

Serves 4 to 6

Caesar Salad

This is a special Caesar dressing—uncommonly thick and creamy, the anchovy and garlic flavors are evenly balanced as they coat. Serve it as a dinner salad or top with grilled chicken, salmon, or steak for a meal.

1 egg yolk
Juice of 1 lemon
½ ounce (4) anchovies
¼ cup, plus 2 teaspoons Dijon mustard
3 cloves garlic
1½ cups extra virgin olive oil
½ cup grated Parmesan cheese
2 teaspoons black pepper
1 pound Romaine lettuce, washed
¼ cup shaved Parmesan cheese
1 cup croutons

Combine egg yolk, lemon juice, anchovies, mustard, and garlic; puree in a food processor or a blender. With machine running, slowly drizzle oil until mixture is the consistency of mayonnaise; drizzling the oil is important to keep the full, creamy texture. Transfer to a bowl; add Parmesan and pepper. Mix thoroughly.

Tear lettuce into bite-size pieces and place in a large bowl. Before serving, toss lettuce with dressing until generously coated; divide onto plates. Top with shaved Parmesan and croutons.

Serves 4

Walnut-Gorgonzola Salad

Served in Percie's Poolside Grill, this is a tart and refreshing favorite.

1 pound mixed greens
1 cup crumbled Gorgonzola cheese
1 cup roasted walnuts
1 cup sliced Granny Smith apples
½ cup sliced red onion
¼ cup balsamic vinegar

Combine greens, Gorgonzola, walnuts, apples, and onion. Toss with balsamic vinegar. Divide between plates and serve.

Serves 4

Heirloom Garden

In the early 1900s a five-acre vegetable garden supplied Chico Hot Springs with fresh produce. Utilizing the thermal water to irrigate rows and rows of plants, Chico owner Percie Knowles grew gargantuan sunflowers and a healthy harvest to be canned for winter months. Fresh strawberries, cabbage, carrots, and an assortment of other vegetables helped Percie serve simple, yet memorable fare.

Today the use of fresh ingredients is essential to Chico's signature menu, so in 1997 the garden was resurrected. Charming and utilitarian, the quarter-acre plot occupies a sunny spot to the east of the main lodge. Walking paths and benches welcome guests to enjoy and explore. Thermal run-off from the swimming pool still irrigates the summer garden as well as a year-round greenhouse. It's not unusual to see the head chef perusing the rows of herbs for the nightly dinner special or to see the gardeners harvesting spinach for the evening's salads. In the summer months, Chico's garden yields most of the greens for salads, as well as herbs to make soups, sauces, seasoning, and garnishes.

Bill Tolbet, the head gardener at Chico

Inside the climate-controlled greenhouse the lush canopy of a healthy passionflower plant hangs from the rafters. A banana tree grows in the corner. Though neither plant bears fruit, they both thrive in this environment; the passionflowers are a spectacular visual addition to dessert or salad plates. During winter months a perennial garden has been cultivated to provide cut flowers for each table in the dining room. In spring the greenhouse is filled with seedlings that will be planted in summer beds or hanging baskets.

Chico's garden is a great success. It is a testimonial to the resort's pioneer beginnings and agricultural history, as well as to the kitchen's demand for quality ingredients. The garden is as much a novelty as it is a necessity at Chico.

Chico's Ghost

The gravestone at the old Chico cemetery reads: Percie Matheson Knowles, 1860–1941. Loving wife and mother.

Yet some believe that Percie Knowles, the first proprietor of Chico Hot Springs, is still alive—at least in spirit.

Mysterious tales of a prim-looking older woman who appears in the historic hotel on late winter nights have prevailed for the last twenty years. She's said to wear a high collared, long-sleeve dress with her hair pulled back into a tight bun. She smells of lilacs. She doesn't smile or speak.

In 1900 Percie and her husband, Bill Knowles, opened Chico Warm Springs Hotel. Bill was known in the community for his gregarious nature and love of the outdoors. Against his wife's wishes, he bolstered Chico's business with a saloon and lively dance hall. Percie was remembered for her strong opinions against drinking and gambling.

Following her husband's death in 1910, Percie shut down the saloon and transformed Chico into a hospital. She hired a well-known physician and touted the natural hot springs as a cure for everything from "rheumatism to kidney troubles." For thirteen years the health care center thrived, until the doctor's retirement.

When Percie's own health began to suffer, the business faltered even more. She began to pass the hours sitting in a rocking chair in her favorite room on the third floor of the hotel with a view of Emigrant Peak.

Today, stories of Percie's stern ways still pass through the halls at Chico, carried by a ghostly breeze that billows through the curtains in a room where no windows are open. There are countless reports of pots and pans rattling in the kitchen at odd hours; doors slamming in deserted hallways; apparitions that float above the pool; and of a certain rocking chair in a third floor room that is always found facing the window overlooking Emigrant Peak.

Percie Knowles, 1919

Mixed Greens with Orange-Ginger Vinaigrette

One of the all-time most requested Chico recipes, guests rave about the dressing on this salad. It's simple, sweet, and refreshing. Through the years it has become a nostalgic favorite. For best flavor, prepare the vinaigrette a day or two in advance of serving this salad.

Orange-Ginger Vinaigrette:

  Zest and juice of ½ orange
  2 tablespoons minced fresh ginger
  Juice of ½ lemon
  1 cup red wine vinegar
  2 teaspoons ground black pepper
  ¼ cup orange juice concentrate
  ½ cup sugar
  1 cup canola oil
  ½ cup extra virgin olive oil

  1 pound mixed greens
  1 carrot, peeled and grated
  2 tomatoes, quartered
  ¼ cup sliced scallions
  1 cup croutons

To prepare Orange-Ginger Vinaigrette: Combine zest and juice of half an orange, ginger, lemon juice, red wine vinegar, black pepper, orange juice concentrate, and sugar in a blender, turn to high speed. Combine canola and olive oils; while machine is running, drizzle in oil mixture slowly. Let dressing sit at room temperature for one to two days.

Arrange greens on individual serving plates. Top with carrots, tomatoes, scallions, and croutons. Top with Orange-Ginger Vinaigrette.

Serves 4

Shrimp and Purple Cabbage Salad

This uncomplicated salad has a little zing from the garden when served on a bed of arugula. It makes a nice dinner salad or even a colorful summer side dish. For a milder version, it can be served without the arugula.

1 pound medium shrimp
¼ cup mayonnaise
1 teaspoon fresh dill
1 cup chopped purple cabbage
Juice of 1 lemon, plus lemon slices for garnish
½ cup chopped chives
½ pound arugula

Mix shrimp, mayonnaise, dill, cabbage, lemon juice, and chives thoroughly, chill and serve over a bed of arugula with extra slices of lemon for garnish.

Serves 4

French Onion Soup

It is hard to beat this timeless classic—sweet onions sautéed and simmered in brandy, then topped with bubbling Parmesan cheese. It is a wonderful autumn preparation and a lovely beginning to a hearty meal. Prepare the Beef Stock a day in advance.

3 large yellow onions, julienned
1½ tablespoons extra virgin olive oil
1 cup brandy
2 teaspoons minced garlic
½ cup sugar
1 tablespoon salt
2 teaspoons black pepper
6 cups Beef Stock (recipe page 111)
1 cup grated Parmesan cheese
4 Crostini (½-inch-thick) (recipe page 112)

Sauté onions with olive oil in a large stock pot until caramelized. Add brandy; reduce until almost dry. Add garlic, sugar, salt, pepper, and Beef Stock. Simmer for 30 minutes. Remove from heat.

Preheat oven to 400°. Place 4 oven-safe bowls or single-serving crocks on a baking sheet (to catch overflow). Fill each bowl almost to the brim with soup and place Crostini on top; cover with cheese. Bake in the oven until cheese browns slightly (about 10 to 15 minutes) and serve.

Serves 4

Roasted Red Pepper Soup

The earthy flavors of roasted peppers bring out the savory freshness of this soup. The color is a vibrant red that makes any table stunning. This soup is versatile enough to be paired with a variety of other ingredients—try steamed mussels, clams, or other shellfish as a last-minute topping. Prepare Chicken Stock a day in advance.

  6 to 8 large red bell peppers
  2 quarts (64 ounces) Chicken Stock (recipe page 111)
  Canola oil to coat the pan
  2 large yellow onions, peeled, sliced for sautéing
  1 large carrot, rough diced
  4 large shallots, rough diced
  32 ounces (4 cups) canned tomatoes with juice, or 6 large tomatoes, peeled and seeded
  4 stalks celery, rough diced
  2 cloves garlic, rough diced
  1 cup sherry (such as Gallo), divided
  1 cup heavy whipping cream
  ¼ teaspoon saffron
  Juice of 1 lemon
  ½ teaspoon of your favorite hot sauce (optional)
  Salt and pepper to taste
  ½ cup grated Parmesan cheese

Roast whole red bell peppers over an open flame on a gas burning stovetop or grill; remove from flame when skin is mostly blackened and immerse in an ice bath to remove skin easily. Seed and dice. Peppers can also be roasted in 400-degree oven for 10 to 20 minutes. Set aside.

In a large soup pot, warm Chicken Stock on medium-high heat until boiling. Add roasted red peppers; let simmer.

Heat a saucepan with canola oil and sauté onion, carrot, shallots, tomatoes, celery, and garlic until browned. Add ½ cup sherry to vegetables, deglazing the pan. Stir and combine with hot chicken stock. On medium-high heat allow mixture to reduce to half, about 1½ hours, stirring occasionally.

Puree mixture in a blender or food processor until smooth. Return to soup pot on low heat. Whisk in heavy whipping cream, saffron, lemon juice, remaining ½ cup sherry, and the optional hot sauce. Add salt and pepper to your taste, simmer for 10 minutes, and serve with freshly grated Parmesan cheese.

Serves 4

Seafood Bisque

This light, creamy soup is an easy backdrop for the wonderful flavors of lobster and shrimp. The tomato paste provides a lovely color and a tangy flavor here.

2 small lobster tails (5 ounces each)
1 dozen large shrimp
2 shallots, diced
4 tablespoons (½ stick) unstalted butter
¼ cup white wine or sherry
4 cups Shrimp Stock (recipe page 114)
¼ cup tomato paste
1 pint heavy whipping cream
1 tablespoon heaping chopped fresh dill
1 tablespoon chopped parsley, plus more for garnish
2 tablespoons paprika
2 teaspoons seafood base
Juice of 1 lemon
Salt and white pepper to taste
Cornstarch (optional)
4 Crostini (recipe page 112)

Clean and shell lobster and shrimp; reserve shells for stock. Set aside seafood until just before serving. Prepare stock.

In a large stockpot, sauté shallots in butter until sweated, add white wine or sherry, and shrimp stock. Whisk tomato paste into stock until combined. Bring to a boil over medium-high heat. Add cream, dill, parsley, paprika, and seafood base, whisking lightly. Simmer for 20 minutes on medium heat, making sure it does not boil or cream will scald. Add lemon juice, salt and white pepper to taste. Thicken with cornstarch and water (follow instructions on cornstarch container) to desired consistency. Simmer on low until ready to serve.

Steam shelled lobster tails over boiling water until edges appear red and meat is white (about 5 minutes). Then steam shrimp in same pot until they turn pink. Slice lobsters into half-inch-thick medallions, divide between shallow serving bowls; ladle soup over lobster. Place Crostini and three shrimp per bowl on top of soup and garnish with a sprinkling of chopped parsley.

Serves 4

Gazpacho

On a hot summer day, a cold soup is a wonderful thirst quencher.
Using herbs fresh from the garden, this rendition is both sweet and spicy.

8 very ripe Roma tomatoes, rough chopped
3 stalks celery, rough chopped
2 large English cucumbers, peeled, seeded, and rough chopped
1 large yellow pepper, seeded, ribbed, and rough chopped
1 medium jalapeno, seeded, ribbed, and rough chopped
8 scallions, rough chopped
½ cup balsamic vinegar
1 tablespoon salt
½ cup extra virgin olive oil
2 cups tomato juice
¼ cup parsley
2 tablespoons chopped parsley
2 tablespoons chopped arugula
2 tablespoons chopped cilantro
Whole chives for garnish

1 dozen medium shrimp, cleaned and steamed (optional)
1 lemon, quartered into wedges (optional)

Marinate tomatoes, celery, cucumbers, peppers, and scallions with vinegar and salt overnight in the refrigerator.

Mix olive oil and tomato juice together in a separate container. Pour 1 cup of marinated vegetables in a food processor or blender, pulse while drizzling about ¼ cup olive oil/tomato mixture for 30 to 60 seconds; mixture should be blended but still slightly chunky. Pour each batch into a clean bowl and repeat until finished. Once processed, add parsley, arugula, and cilantro; chill.

Garnish with whole chives and serve with steamed shrimp and lemon wedges on the side.

Serves 4

Smoked Chicken and Corn Chowder

A specialty of banquet chef Craig Flick, this zesty soup is an amalgam of smoky chicken and spicy fresh ingredients. There are two tricks that make this soup exceptional. First is the smoked chicken, it elevates the heartiness well beyond your mother's chicken soup. Smoked chicken is available at many grocery stores or at fine butcher shops. Second is the addition of sour cream at the end of the recipe. Whisking it into the broth changes the consistency of the soup, adding a richness that is subtle rather than overpowering. Prepare Chicken Stock a day in advance.

2 Anaheim peppers
2 cups frozen corn kernels or 12 ears fresh corn
2 quarts (64 ounces) Chicken Stock (recipe page 111)
Canola oil to coat bottom of pan for vegetable sauté
1 white onion, diced
1 red onion, diced
1 bunch green onions, diced
3 stalks celery, diced
2 shallots, diced
2 tablespoons chopped garlic
1 jalapeno, diced
½ pound red potatoes, diced with skins on
1 red bell pepper, diced
1 green bell pepper, diced
1 yellow bell pepper, diced
⅓ cup chopped parsley
½ cup dark beer
4 medium flour tortillas
¼ cup canola oil
2 teaspoons favorite hot sauce, such as Cholula or Tabasco (optional)
Salt and pepper to taste
1 whole smoked chicken or 3 smoked chicken breasts, diced
½ cup sour cream
Zest of ½ lime
2 tablespoons lime juice
¼ cup chopped fresh cilantro

Roast Anaheim peppers over an open flame on a gas burning stovetop or grill; remove

from flame when skin is mostly blackened and immerse in an ice bath to remove skin easily. Seed and dice. Peppers can also be roasted in 400-degree oven for 10 to 20 minutes. Set aside.

Preheat oven to 400°. Pour corn kernels on an ungreased baking sheet and roast in oven for 10 to 20 minutes until slightly brown. If using fresh corn, roast it on a grill until brown while still on the cob, then slice kernels off. Set aside.

In a large soup pot, warm Chicken Stock on medium heat and simmer. In a large pan coated with canola oil, sauté all onions, celery, shallots, garlic, jalapeno, potatoes, all bell peppers, and parsley over medium-high heat until onions are translucent. Don't worry if vegetables stick to pan; this will give the soup more intense flavor. Season with salt and pepper to taste; be conservative with the pepper, as the jalapeno and optional hot sauce make this a spicy soup.

Add dark beer to deglaze the pan with vegetables, stir and allow to reduce for about 15 minutes. Combine roasted corn kernels with warm chicken stock, then add sautéed vegetables; bring to a boil. Simmer for approximately one hour; do not stir soup.

Cut four flour tortillas (or corn if you prefer) into long strips, ¼-inch thick. Heat ¼ cup canola oil in a saucepan until almost smoking. Add tortilla strips and fry until crispy. Set aside for later as garnish on top of soup.

After one hour, stir soup; add optional hot sauce and salt and pepper to your taste. Right before serving add diced chicken, roasted Anaheim peppers, and sour cream. Whisk the soup until sour cream is blended and reaches a very light, creamy consistency. Add lime zest and juice; bring to a boil again before serving and garnish with crisp tortilla strips.

Serves 4 to 6

Wild Mushroom Bisque

Spring brings morels and other wild mushrooms bursting from the forest floors throughout the region. If you are lucky you might catch a string of special dishes on the dining room menu prepared with an assortment of fresh fungi. This is the best of those savory recipes, though it can also be prepared with dried mushrooms. Prepare Chicken Stock a day in advance.

¼ pound fresh portobello mushrooms, grilled and chopped
¼ pound fresh oyster mushrooms, stemmed and chopped
2 large leeks, cleaned and chopped
½ large yellow onion, chopped
2 tablespoons minced garlic
½ cup sherry or white wine
2 quarts (64 ounces) Chicken Stock (recipe page 111)
2 cups heavy whipping cream
¼ pound fresh morel mushrooms
2 tablespoons unsalted butter
1 teaspoon fresh thyme leaves, plus extra sprigs for garnish
Salt and pepper to taste
Crostini (recipe page 112)
¼ cup grated Parmesan cheese

In a large stock pot, sauté fresh oyster and grilled portobello mushrooms, leeks, onion, and garlic until soft. Add sherry or wine, Chicken Stock, and cream; simmer on medium heat until reduced by one-third (about 45 minutes). Puree and return to pot. Sauté whole morels in butter, add 1 teaspoon thyme leaves, salt and pepper to taste. Serve soup with Crostini and top with sautéed morels, Parmesan, and extra sprigs of thyme for garnish.

Serves 4 to 6

Summer Vegetable Medley

Sweet corn and tender asparagus make an unlikely match, but here they offer bursts of fun yellow-green color on the dinner plate and, oddly, a complementary medley of flavors.

3 ears fresh corn
1 to 2 pounds fresh asparagus
8 tablespoons (1 stick) butter
2 tablespoons fresh thyme leaves
Juice of 1 lemon
½ cup scallions, sliced into rounds

Cut corn into 2-inch pieces, about three slices per ear. Steam or boil until three-quarters cooked, still crunchy. Remove from heat and set aside.

Trim asparagus to 3 or 4-inch long spears. In a saucepan, melt butter. Add thyme leaves, lemon juice, and scallions; sauté for one minute. Add asparagus and sauté until still crunchy. Arrange hot corn on serving platter or individual plates, place asparagus on top, and drizzle with herb butter from pan.

Serves 4

Gorgonzola Au Gratin

Served hot out of the oven or chilled overnight in the refrigerator, this is the perfect potato dish. Prepared with several layers of thin-sliced potatoes and a savory gorgonzola cheese mixture, it is a versatile complement to meat, poultry, or fish.

1 large leek, cleaned and sliced
1 tablespoon minced garlic
¼ cup chopped raisins
½ cup crumbled Gorgonzola cheese
2 cups heavy whipping cream
1 teaspoon salt
1 teaspoon black pepper
5 to 6 peeled Idaho potatoes, sliced thin

Combine all ingredients except potatoes in a saucepan; simmer until thick. Remove from heat.

Preheat oven to 350°. In a greased 9-inch pie pan or decorative baking dish of similar proportion, begin laying potatoes along the bottom of pan so there is a little overlapping, but no surface area showing. Spread a thin coating of cheese and leek mixture, followed by another layer of potatoes. Press down and squeeze out any air bubbles every few layers. Your last layer should be topped with cheese and leek mixture. Cover with aluminum foil and bake for 1½ hours until potatoes are tender. Let cool over night before cutting. This dish can be reheated at a low temperature, about 200° for 15 minutes to serve warm, or it can be served cold for a picnic.

Serves 6

Pine Nut Crusted Halibut ▶

Main Courses

Pine Nut Crusted Halibut

(see photo page 51)

This long-time favorite is a famous example of Chico's style of "layering" flavors. Here, with fresh halibut flown in twice a week, we offset the flaky, white fish with a heavy coating of pine nuts and deep buttery sauce. But to lighten up the ensemble we add a medley of crisp fruit and vegetables. Fresh halibut runs seasonally, but this recipe can also work with other firm, white fish, such as sole. The Port Wine Butter Sauce cannot be reheated or chilled, so prepare it while the halibut is in the oven or just before serving.

Pine Nut Crust:
> 2 cups pine nuts
> ¾ cup bread crumbs
> 1 teaspoon salt
> ⅓ cup parsley

Halibut:
> 1 cup buttermilk
> ½ cup flour
> 4 (6-ounce) halibut fillets
>
> Port Wine Butter Sauce (recipe page 113)
> 2 cups Mango Salsa (recipe page 113)

To prepare Pine Nut Crust: In a food processor, add all the ingredients. Pulse until nuts are diced, but not too fine; remove and set aside. You can also prepare the crust by hand. Be sure to dice the nuts before combining with other ingredients.

To prepare Halibut: Preheat the oven to 400°. Place buttermilk, flour, and pine nut mixture in separate bowls and arrange in a line on the counter. Take fillets and dip one side only in flour, buttermilk, then pine nut crust. On the stove heat a pan with a touch of olive oil and with crust-side down sauté the fish until nuts are golden brown. Place the sautéed fish on a greased baking dish, bare fish–side down and bake in the oven for 8 to 10 minutes. Present the halibut in a pool of Port Wine Butter Sauce, topped with the fresh Mango Salsa.

Serves 4

Vegetable Tower

Assembling this dish is an art, each layer locks in flavors of grilled vegetables and creamy goat cheese. It is a vegetarian option in the restaurant, but this recipe is so versatile that it can be used as an appetizer served with Crostini (recipe page 112) or even as a side dish to accompany a main course.

marinade:
- 3 sprigs fresh rosemary
- 3 sprigs fresh thyme
- 2 lemons, cut in half
- 4 tablespoons minced garlic
- 4 cups extra virgin olive oil
- 1 teaspoon salt
- 1 tablespoon black pepper

- 3 semi-ripe beefsteak tomatoes, sliced in ½-inch-thick rings
- 2 medium red onions, sliced into rings
- 2 large eggplants, sliced into rings
- 1 bunch asparagus, stems cut off
- 2 large zucchini, cut lengthwise
- 8 ounces goat cheese
- ½ cup Balsamic Vinegar Reduction Sauce (recipe page 110)
- ½ cup Basil Oil (recipe page 110)

To prepare marinade: Mix all marinade ingredients together, squeezing juice from lemons. Add sliced vegetables and toss until all are coated with oil. Marinate for at least 2 hours at room temperature.

Remove vegetables from marinade and grill until soft but not charred or mushy. Vegetables such as tomatoes and zucchini will finish before others, so check throughout grilling; remove cooked pieces.

Drizzle individual oversized plates generously with alternating lines of Basil Oil and Balsamic Vinegar Reduction Sauce. On top of the sauce, build four individual towers with eggplant, onion, tomato, and zucchini, in that order, sprinkling crumbled goat cheese between each vegetable layer. Arrange asparagus in a fan around the base of the tower on the plate, top with more goat cheese crumbles and serve. You can also build the towers on one large serving platter depending on the occasion.

Serves 4

Chico Mixed Grille

This nightly offering changes regularly and features contrasting, but complementary preparations of wild game, fowl, and seafood. It can be a sampling of regular menu items, such as the Pine Nut Crusted Halibut (recipe page 52) and the Duck L'Orange (recipe page 58). It can be a combination of native game, such as bison, elk, and quail. Often it is a medley of wonderful earthy flavors that make for a distinct meal. Here is one rendition from our kitchen, but don't be afraid to fuse other recipes from this book to make a better mix for your own kitchen.

Grilled Antelope Medallions:
    1½ cups red wine
    ¼ cup chopped fresh thyme
    ¼ cup chopped fresh savory
    ¼ cup chopped fresh marjoram
    1 tablespoon cracked peppercorn
    1 teaspoon sea salt
    2 large shallots, rough chopped
    1 tablespoon whole grain Dijon mustard
    2 tablespoons red wine vinegar
    2½ pounds antelope tenderloin, sliced into 1-inch-thick medallions

Combine wine, spices, shallots, mustard, and vinegar in a large pan. Add sliced antelope and marinate in the refrigerator for at least 6 hours. Grill to desired temperature.

Roasted Pheasant:
   1 teaspoon kosher salt
   Black pepper to taste
   2 cloves garlic, sliced
   ¼ cup chopped fresh thyme
   ¼ cup chopped fresh sage
   ¼ cup chopped fresh basil
   ¼ cup chopped fresh oregano
   2 cups, plus 2 tablespoons olive oil
   2 lemons
   4 large pheasant, cut into quarters

In a bowl, combine salt, pepper, garlic, and herbs. In a large pan, heat the 2 cups olive oil on high heat until almost smoking; pour over herbs. Stir until combined and let sit for one minute. Juice lemons and pour into herb oil. Remove any remaining seeds from lemon rinds, and add rinds to herb oil. Place pheasant in herb oil; marinate in refrigerator for at least 3 hours.

Preheat oven to 350°. Heat a large pan and add the 2 tablespoons olive oil with pheasant. Fry until skin on all pieces is golden, turning often. Place pheasant in a baking dish and bake for 15 to 20 minutes. Test the thickest piece for doneness.

Arrange prepared antelope and pheasant freshly cooked or warm on a platter or individual serving plates, garnish with fresh herbs.

Serves 4

Grilled Ahi with Thai Onion Sauté

With fresh fish flown in several times a week, this East-meets-West dish is possible even in rural Montana. Light, tangy, and spicy, it's a favorite special in the dining room. This dish is nice served on a bed of cooked Asian noodles, such as rice stick or Soba.

Thai Onion Sauté:
    1 large leek, cleaned and julienned
    1 large red onion, julienned
    ¾ cup Thai Vinaigrette (recipe page 33)

    4 (8-ounce) yellowfin tuna fillets (also excellent with mahimahi)
    Salt and pepper to taste

To prepare Thai Onion Sauté: Sauté leek and onion until soft; add vinaigrette and cook until all liquid is almost absorbed dry.

Season tuna with salt and pepper. Grill for 2 to 3 minutes on each side to serve rare; top with Thai Onion Sauté.

Serves 4

Duck L'Orange

(see photo page 57)

Chef Larry Edwards meticulously perfected this Chico classic in the mid-1970s. The crispy skin of the duck seals in the moistness of its dark, rich meat. The most challenging aspect of this recipe is the Grand Marnier Sauce; it requires several hours to prepare. The sweet glaze featured here is excellent on its own, but the Grand Marnier Sauce adds yet another layer of flavor. Make the sauce one or two days in advance for best results.

  2 grade A Muscovy whole ducks
  2 tablespoons chopped fresh rosemary
  2 tablespoons chopped fresh thyme
  1 tablespoon kosher salt
  1 tablespoon black pepper
  Peels of 4 oranges, discard oranges
  1¼ cups water

glaze:
  2 cups honey
  2 cups orange juice concentrate

Grand Marnier Sauce:
  1 cinnamon stick
  1 star of anise
  1 teaspoon coriander
  1 orange, peeled
  2½ tablespoons honey
  2½ tablespoons raspberry vinegar
  ½ cup orange juice concentrate
  ¾ gallon Dark Duck Stock (recipe page 112)
  1 teaspoon orange zest
  1 bay leaf
  ¼ cup Grand Marnier or orange liqueur
  5 shallots, peeled, sliced thick
  ¼ cup mandarin orange segments

To prepare ducks: Preheat oven to 275°. Cut off fat around rear of duck, remove tail bone and skin around neck. Save fat and skin to be rendered. Mix all spices together. Roll orange peels in 1 cup water then spices; insert two peels into the body cavity of each duck. Rub remaining spices across duck breast. Roast duck, back down, for 1 hour and 45 minutes. Let cool, remove rib cage and backbone leaving four duck halves.

Render fat and skin in a saucepan with ¼ cup water. Simmer for 20 minutes until water has evaporated and all that remains is beautiful duck oil. Set aside.

To glaze ducks: Preheat oven to 400°. Combine honey and orange juice concentrate. Bring to a boil; remove from heat and set aside. In a large sauté pan, bring duck oil to a fairly warm temperature, not boiling. Place one half duck in pan skin side down and cook until skin is crispy. Use a metal spatula to remove from pan with skin intact, and place in a deep roasting pan. Repeat with other duck halves. In the roasting pan, pour half a cup of glaze on each duck half. Bake, basting duck every 4 minutes until honey becomes thick enough to coat the skin. Serve hot and crispy.

To make Grand Marnier Sauce: On the stovetop, toast cinnamon stick, anise, and coriander in a large stockpot over medium heat until brown, about 7 minutes, shaking contents in pot occasionally to keep from burning. Add orange, honey, raspberry vinegar, and orange juice concentrate. Reduce until honey becomes thick (up to 1 hour). Add stock, orange zest, and bay leaf. Reduce over medium-high heat until thick (up to 6 hours). When it thickens to the consistency of thin gravy, add Grand Marnier. Let simmer 10 minutes. Strain and return to clean pot to simmer while roasting shallots.

Roast shallots at 400° for 10 to 15 minutes. Combine shallots and mandarin segments; serve on the side with duck. Serve sauce hot on the side in individual ramekins.

Serves 4

Yellowstone Chicken

With the Yellowstone River just minutes from Chico, it's easy to handpick perfectly round, well-worn rocks. The truth is that any rock will do. In this recipe the chicken is baked at a high temperature to seal in the moisture and flavors of thyme and rosemary. The rocks facilitate the short cooking time without sacrificing flavor. In the restaurant we use farm-raised Hutterite chickens from nearby Martinsdale, a colony of Anabaptist farmers.

4 very smooth, round rocks, about 5 inches in diameter
2 tablespoons fresh thyme
2 tablespoons fresh rosemary
8 tablespoons extra virgin olive oil
1 teaspoon salt
1 tablespoon black pepper
2 whole chickens, backbone removed and split in half

Preheat oven to 400°. Place rocks in oven while it is preheating, and continue to preheat the rocks for 15 minutes after the oven comes to temperature. Combine herbs, oil, salt, and pepper. Arrange poultry on a 9 x 12-inch oven-proof baking dish. Remove rocks from oven with tongs. Using tongs, place a rock under thigh of each half chicken; the rock should be snugly tucked into the skin and meat. Drizzle chickens with olive oil mixture. Bake for 25 to 30 minutes until the chicken has reached 165° on a meat thermometer. Serve the chicken with the rock intact; it gives the dish a nice presentation by making the chicken stand tall on the plate.

Serves 4

Shrimp Chesapeake

The heavy flavors of crab, shrimp, and Hollandaise Sauce are pleasantly balanced by this light Fresh Citrus Vinaigrette. As you prepare the shrimp, it's important to cut a little deeper when butterflying so that the Chesapeake Crab Mix can sit well. Save any leftover crab mix to make crab cakes; simply shape into patties and sauté in butter until lightly crisp on the outside.

Chesapeake Crab Mix:
   2 celery stalks, diced
   ½ large yellow onion, diced
   ¼ red bell pepper, diced
   ¼ green bell pepper, diced
   1 garlic clove, diced
   2 tablespoons unsalted butter
   1 cup seasoned bread crumbs
   3 tablespoons mayonnaise
   1 teaspoon Worcestershire sauce
   Juice of ½ lemon
   1 teaspoon Old Bay Seasoning
   1 egg
   ½ pound fine crab meat, (fine canned crab is available in most stores) drain excess water

   2 pounds medium or large shrimp, deveined and butterflied
   ¼ to ½ cup white wine
   1 cup Hollandaise Sauce (recipe page 113)
   1 cup Fresh Citrus Vinaigrette (recipe page 112)

Sauté celery, onion, bell peppers, and garlic in butter just until onion is translucent. Add to a bowl with bread crumbs, mayonnaise, Worcestershire, lemon juice, Old Bay, egg, and crab; mix well. The mixture should not have any excess liquid from the egg, it should be stiff.

Using a tablespoon or a soup spoon heaped with crab mix, place on the bottom side of the butterflied shrimp. The largest part of the shrimp will lay flat and the tail should curl over the top of stuffing. Gently press and shape the crab mix into a ball on the shrimp.

Preheat oven to 450°. Arrange the shrimp in a baking dish. Add just a little white wine to cover the bottom of the pan, not the shrimp. Add a dollop of Hollandaise Sauce on each shrimp and bake for 10 minutes. The topping should be golden brown; peek under the crab mix on one shrimp to make sure it is cooked completely. Ladle about ½ ounce of Fresh Citrus Vinaigrette on the dinner plates and place the cooked shrimp on top.

Serves 4

Rosemary Rack of Lamb
with Basil-Mint Jelly

As with so many of Chico's preparations fresh ingredients are essential, this traditional rack of lamb entrée is no exception. Utilizing garden herbs—rosemary, basil, and mint—the local lamb is marinated for two days to soak up those fresh flavors. A hazelnut crust accents the meat's naturally rich flavor, while the clean sweetness of Basil-Mint Jelly cleanses the palate with each bite. Prepare Basil-Mint Jelly at least one day in advance of using it in this recipe.

marinade:
> 6 cups extra virgin olive oil
> 10 large shallots peeled and sliced
> 10 cloves of garlic, rough chopped
> 2 lemons, sliced
> 4 sprigs fresh rosemary
> 3 bay leaves
> 2 tablespoons peppercorn mélange
>
> 4 (9-ounce) racks of lamb

crust:
> 1 cup hazelnuts
> 2 tablespoons fresh rosemary leaves
> 1 cup bread crumbs
> ½ tablespoon salt
>
> 1 cup Basil-Mint Jelly (recipe page 110)

Temperature Chart:	
Rare	6 to 8 minutes
Medium rare	8 to 12 minutes
Medium	12 to 16 minutes
Medium well	16 to 18 minutes
Well	20 minutes

To prepare marinade: Combine all ingredients in a large container and marinate lamb racks for two days before cooking.

To prepare crust: Place all ingredients in a food processor; process until hazelnuts are rough chopped. You can also prepare this by hand; chop nuts and rosemary then combine other ingredients.

Preheat oven to 400°. Remove lamb from marinade and press crust on bottom side of rack loin (the side with the most meat). Roast to desired temperature.

Serve Basil-Mint Jelly on the side for dipping or spreading with each bite of prepared lamb.

Serves 4

Sole En Croute
with Fresh Citrus Vinaigrette

You can use whimsy as inspiration in finishing this recipe. It calls for the pastry to be cut in the shape of a fish, so imagine it is a fat trout you had on the line in the Yellowstone River. Get creative, add eyes, fins, scales, facets of the tail; the result will be a fun design, accompanied by seriously delicious flavors.

4 (10 x 15-inch) puffed pastry sheets, thawed
4 (6-ounce) Dover sole fillets (substitute halibut or any white fish)
8 ounces Chesapeake Crab Mix (recipe page 61)
½ cup white wine
Juice of 1 lemon
Salt and pepper to taste
Old Bay Seasoning to taste
1 egg
¼ cup heavy whipping cream

1 cup Fresh Citrus Vinaigrette (recipe page 112)
2 cups Mango Salsa (recipe page 113)

Slice the pastry sheets in half widthwise, then place half sheets on top of each other (you will have four stacks of two sheets). Cut out a shape of a fish (or an oval similar to the shape of a football); reserve excess pieces of pastry to add other fun features such as the tail or scales and fins. Repeat this three more times with each pastry sheet pair. Try to judge the size of your filling. Your pastry should come out the size of half a dinner plate to allow room for a starch and a side dish.

Once each pastry is cut like a fish, separate the pieces and place them side by side on a flat surface. Choose one piece in each fish/oval shape pair as the "bottom"; place one fillet on each chosen bottom pastry piece. Pressing down gently on the fillet, fan out the fish, leaving a ¼-inch space around the edge of the pastry. Spoon 2 ounces of Chesapeake Crab Mix on the fillet, spreading it to the edges of the fish meat with splash of white wine and splash of lemon juice. Sprinkle with salt, pepper, and Old Bay Seasoning. Top with the remaining fish-shape piece of pastry, stretching out over the fillet and Crab Mix to meet edges of bottom pastry. Pinch edges together to seal. Repeat this three more times with remaining cut pastry pairs.

After sealing the edges of the your filled pastries, add finishing touches using excess pieces of pastry to create fun features such as the tail or scales and fins. For scales on the body of your fish-shaped pastry, cut tiny half-moon shapes in the surface of the dough; be careful not to cut through pastry. This does two things, it adds a decorative flair and it provides venting for the puffed pastry so that no air bubbles form during baking. Shape leftover dough into eyes and mouth, fins and tails. Have fun with this part, though you can also skip the decorating and just get the goods in the oven.

Preheat oven to 450°. Whisk egg and heavy whipping cream together to prepare egg wash. Place pastry fillets on greased baking dish and brush with egg wash. Bake for approximately 15 minutes. Pastry should be golden brown all over. Remove from oven. It will be tempting to dig in immediately, but for best results allow your masterpiece to set for up to 15 minutes. Serve with Citrus Vinaigrette on the side and Mango Salsa.

Serves 4

Frenched Pork Chop with Cornbread Stuffing and Apple Chutney

Melding rich autumn flavors of sweet apple and spicy chilies, this pork takes on a sumptuously rustic refinement. Cut like a rack of lamb, this recipe adds a decorative flair to pork. A local butcher or even a grocery store meat department will prepare this cut for you; be sure to request a 1-inch-thick restaurant cut. If this is not available, use a regular pork chop.

4 (10-ounce) Frenched (bone-in) pork chops

Cornbread Stuffing:
    3 slices bacon, chopped
    3 stalks celery, diced
    1 large carrot, peeled and diced
    1 medium white onion, diced
    ½ cup Madeira wine or sweet sherry
    ¼ cup heavy whipping cream
    ¼ cup dried cranberries
    2 tablespoons chopped fresh sage
    4 cups chopped Maple Cornbread (recipe page 107)

Apple Chutney:
    2 cups apple juice concentrate
    2 tablespoons ancho chiles
    ½ tablespoon cornstarch
    ½ tablespoon hot water
    2 apples (Gala, McIntosh, or Granny Smith), peeled and chopped
    ¼ cup chopped red onion
    ¼ cup seeded and chopped red bell pepper

To make Cornbread Stuffing: Render fat from bacon; add celery, carrot, and onion. Sauté until vegetables are soft; add Madeira, cream, cranberries, sage, and Maple Cornbread. Stir thoroughly until cornbread has soaked up all liquid and mixture sticks together.

Cut a slit into each pork chop, starting at the base of the bone and cutting lengthwise toward the center of the loin. Place ⅓ cup of prepared stuffing into each chop and grill 6 to 10 minutes on each side until pork is cooked to medium well. You can also broil the meat for the same amount of time. Serve with warm Apple Chutney on the side.

To prepare Apple Chutney: Bring apple juice concentrate and chiles to a boil. In a separate container, combine cornstarch and hot water. Once apple juice and chilies begins to boil, add cornstarch mixture. Bring back to a boil and remove from heat. Sauté apples, onion, and pepper until soft; add apple concentrate sauce and stir. Serve warm.

Serves 4

Beef Wellington

This old English recipe is heavy and decadent. Beef tenderloin coated with duck liver paté and wrapped in a buttery puffed pastry—this dish barely needs accoutrements. In the Chico dining room, this signature dish is prepared for two and carved tableside by our servers. The paté is made in-house, using duck liver, pistachios, and cognac; but it is acceptable to use premade paté or even liverwurst if that is all you can find.

    2 (16-ounce) center cut beef tenderloin
    ½ tablespoon sea salt
    1 tablespoon black pepper
    1 tablespoon canola oil, plus more for coating baking dish
    1 (10 x 15-inch) puffed pastry sheet, thawed
    4 ounces duck liver paté (available at specialty food stores, delis, and some grocery
        stores)

Trim the fat and muscle off each tenderloin unless your butcher has already done so. Season the two pieces of meat with salt and pepper. Heat oil in a large skillet over high heat until almost smoking; sear meat until brown on all sides. Remove from pan and set aside.

Preheat oven to 400° and grease a baking dish with oil. Set aside. Cut 10 x 15-inch puff pastry in half. Lay pastry out on a clean flat surface and spread 2 ounces of paté evenly down the middle of both sheets, lengthwise. Place tenderloin on top of paté and fold pastry to enclose meat like a present. The corners of the pastry will be tucked inside and smoothly pressed against the meat. Lay the Wellington, fold-side down, on greased baking dish and bake to desired interior temperature. Allow 30 to 45 minutes cooking time, checking the meat temperature at about 30 minutes; a meat thermometer is essential. Preparing the meat to your desired temperature without undercooking or burning the pastry is what makes this classic recipe tricky. Remember that because the meat is enclosed in pastry it will continue to cook once you remove it from the oven; undercook about five degrees to compensate for this. See the temperature chart for Beef Wellington.

Temperature Chart:	
Rare	90 to 100°
Medium rare	100 to 110°
Medium	110 to 120°
Medium well	120 to 130°

When Wellington is done, let stand 15 to 20 minutes. Slice with a serrated knife and serve.

Serves 4

Grilled New York Strip
with Sundried Tomato Butter

Paradise Valley is cattle country at its richest. So in the restaurant we use only Montana-certified beef. The New York is the quintessential American steak, a robust and rugged cut of beef with an almost rangy flavor that is perfect for grilling. Topped with this compound butter (prepare in advance), the tangy hint of tomatoes bursts in your mouth with each bite.

4 (12-ounce) New York steaks
8 Sundried Tomato Compound Butter patties (recipe page 114)

Grill each steak to desired temperature.

Place two butter patties on each steak and serve.

Serves 4

Temperature Chart:

Rare	2 to 3 minutes on each side
Medium rare	4 to 5 minutes on each side
Medium	6 to 8 minutes on each side
Medium well	10 minutes on each side

Herb Crusted Filet Mignon
with a Port Wine Sauce

Montana is famous for its beef and Chico uses the finest cuts for its menu. The combination of herbs in this recipe brings out the natural, earthy flavors of the most tender meat.

¼ cup fennel seeds
¼ cup whole coriander seeds
1 teaspoon salt
1 teaspoon black pepper
4 (8-ounce) beef tenderloin steaks
Port Wine Sauce (recipe page 113)

In a spice grinder or blender, pulse fennel, coriander seeds, salt, and pepper until coarsely ground. Roll outer edge of each steak in herbs to form a crust; do not encrust cut ends. Grill each steak to desired temperature.

Ladle warm Port Wine Sauce onto individual serving plates making a small pool slightly larger than the steaks; set the steaks on top of the sauce.

Serves 4

Temperature Chart:

Rare	2 to 4 minutes on each side
Medium rare	6 to 8 minutes on each side
Medium	10 to 12 minutes on each side
Medium well	14 to 18 minutes on each side

Chico's Source

"I went down to the hot springs and washed my dirty duds," wrote miner John S. Hackney in his journal dated January 16, 1865.

This is the first written record of the geothermal springs on the southeastern end of Paradise Valley. The camp of miners who settled here during the Montana gold rush utilized the hot water for bathing, cooking, and cleaning. Regional Native American tribes—the Sheepeaters, Crow, Flathead, and Sioux found it centuries before the settlers. But eventually it was an industrious miner, Bill Knowles, who developed Chico as a destination for a relaxing, even healing, soak in the natural, odorless pools.

In 1897, early soakers enjoyed hot, steamy baths

The building that housed "The Plunge" was completed in 1902.

in two wooden, four-foot-deep tubs housed in a wooden shed on the hillside where the water flowed naturally. Later, a 44-foot-wide and six-foot-deep pool was constructed and the water was piped in to fill it. By 1902 "The Plunge," as it was called, was finished; the local newspaper reported that Chico's pools had reached "natatorium status." It featured two indoor oval pools, one six feet deep with the water temperature around 105°, and a larger pool with cooler water for swimming; a second story observer's deck; and private baths for the ladies. Touted as the country's best hot springs, Knowles advertised the "curative powers" of Chico's pools for sufferers of rheumatism, intestinal problems, kidney troubles, as well as skin and blood diseases.

Only once did the water temperature ever falter at Chico, dropping to a low of 85° in 1969. It was discovered that a dam on the fishing pond above the resort had sprung a leak, the cold water overflowed into the hot springs pipe. The problem was promptly fixed and since then Chico's natural pools remain a steady 105° in the small pool and 90° in the larger pool.

Swimmers in the new big pool, July 1919

Desserts

Flathead Cherry Pie

(see photo page 73)

Several hundred miles northwest of Paradise Valley is Montana's banana belt; acres of sweet cherries grow on the shores of Flathead Lake. When the cherries are at their prime in August is the best time to prepare this summer pie. You may substitute any other sweet red cherries in this recipe.

crust:

     6 ounces cream cheese, room temperature
     ½ pound (2 sticks) unsalted butter, softened
     2½ cups all-purpose flour
     ¼ cup milk to brush on top crust

filling:

     2 pounds of Flathead cherries, pitted, stems removed
     1 cup sugar
     ¼ cup cornstarch
     ½ teaspoon salt
     2 tablespoons lemon zest
     ½ teaspoon pure vanilla extract
     2 tablespoons unsalted butter, diced (to dot top of filling in crust)

To prepare crust: Cream the cheese and butter until blended, then add the flour all at once. Mix until a dough ball forms, remove from bowl. Divide into two balls, flatten, and wrap in plastic wrap. Place in the refrigerator until chilled, about 45 minutes to an hour.

To prepare filling: Combine all ingredients except butter in a bowl and toss to coat cherries evenly.

Preheat oven to 350°. Remove one dough round from refrigerator and roll into an 11-inch-diameter circle on a floured surface. Carefully fit into a 9-inch glass pie pan. Moisten edges of bottom crust with water. Fill crust with prepared cherry mixture. Dot pieces of butter on top of the filling. Remove remaining dough round from refrigerator and roll into an 11-inch-diameter circle. Place over top of the filling. Trim edges and gently tuck the top crust under the bottom crust. With your fingers, pinch a decorative edge all the way around the edge. Slice a few small vent holes in the top crust with a sharp knife, being careful not to cut through to the bottom crust. Brush top crust with milk and place pie pan on a baking sheet to catch drippings. Bake pie for 50 minutes until crust is golden. Cool slightly on a wire rack to serve warm or cool completely to serve later; top with vanilla ice cream or whipped cream.

Serves 8

Chico Carrot Cake

The Chico twist—add Mascarpone cheese to the frosting and make a very dense cake.

cake:

  4 eggs
  1½ cups sugar
  ½ cup vegetable oil
  2 cups all-purpose flour
  1½ teaspoons ground cinnamon
  ½ teaspoon baking soda
  ½ teaspoon salt
  4 cups shredded carrots
  1 cup finely chopped walnuts

frosting:

  8 tablespoons (1 stick) unsalted butter, softened
  8 ounces cream cheese, room temperature
  8 ounces Mascarpone cheese, room temperature
  3 cups sifted powdered sugar
  1 tablespoon orange zest
  ¼ teaspoon salt
  ¾ cup finely chopped walnuts

To prepare the cake: Preheat oven to 350°. Grease and flour 2 (9-inch) round cake pans. Whip the eggs and sugar for about 5 minutes, or until the mixture is very thick and pale yellow. Slowly add the oil and whip until combined.

Sift the flour, cinnamon, baking soda, and salt together and whisk to combine. Add to the egg batter and mix until well combined, scraping the sides and bottom of the bowl with a rubber spatula periodically. Fold in carrots and walnuts; this will create a dense mix. Divide and spread the batter into prepared pans and bake until the centers of the cakes spring back when touched with a finger, about 45 to 50 minutes. Cool for 5 minutes on a wire rack; turn cakes out of pans and allow to cool completely.

To prepare the frosting: In an electric mixer on medium speed or by hand, beat the butter, cream cheese, and Mascarpone cheese, scraping the sides and bottom of the bowl with a rubber spatula periodically, until well blended. Add the powdered sugar, zest, and salt; mix for 60 seconds more. Do not overmix or the frosting will not spread easily.

When cakes are cool, place one layer on a serving plate and spread top with a layer of frosting. Place remaining cake on top. Frost the top and sides of entire cake. Press walnuts around the sides. Serve chilled.

Serves 12

Grandma Irene's Chocolate Roulade

When Mike and Eve Art bought Chico Hot Springs in 1973, they worked the property as a family. Eve's mother, who became known to folks in Paradise Valley as well as to guests from near and far as "Grandma Irene," produced this sophisticated European dessert. It graced the dessert table nightly for many years and was a huge success.

filling:
　　2¼ cups (1 pint) heavy whipping cream
　　3 teaspoons melted semisweet chocolate
　　1 teaspoon instant espresso coffee

cake:
　　4 eggs, separated
　　⅓ cup powdered sugar
　　3½ ounces semisweet chocolate, softened (barely melted)
　　¼ cup cake flour
　　2 tablespoons ground almonds

　　2 tablespoons unsalted butter, melted
　　3 tablespoons powdered sugar
　　¼ cup sliced almonds (for garnish)

To prepare filling: Prepare filling in advance. Combine all ingredients and bring to a boil three or four times; take care to remove from heat as it comes to a boil. Cool in an ice bath by transferring to a clean bowl and placing it in a larger bowl filled with ice and water.

When cool, whisk the mixture by hand or with an electric mixer until it is the consistency of whipped cream. Refrigerate for one hour.

To prepare cake: Mix egg yolks with sugar until smooth and creamy. Add softened chocolate. Cream well. Add beaten egg whites alternately with flour and ground almonds.

Preheat oven to 350°. Line a baking sheet (with edges) with wax paper or parchment and brush with melted butter. Pour cake batter into baking sheet and spread evenly. Bake for 15 minutes. Remove from oven and invert onto a towel sprinkled with 1 tablespoon powdered sugar. Strip off wax or parchment paper. Using the towel to keep the cake from sticking together, roll it tightly; the towel will be inside the cake, creating layers that will later be made of filling. This old-fashioned towel trick will make the cake easier to roll up with the filling. Let sit for 30 minutes.

Montana Mud Pie

In the restaurant, we use locally made Wilcoxsons Ice Cream, a 100-year-old company in Livingston. For an extra rich version, we use their specialty flavor, Moose Tracks—vanilla ice cream swirled with semisweet chocolate and mixed with miniature chocolate-covered peanut butter cups. You can buy Wilcoxsons in Montana, Wyoming, and Idaho. Substitute Moose Tracks or your favorite flavor for each of the layers in this recipe.

4 cups chocolate cream-filled chocolate cookies, such as Oreos
5 tablespoons unsalted butter
1 cup crushed toffee
3 cups coffee ice cream, slightly softened
3 cups vanilla ice cream
1½ cups heavy whipping cream
1 pound semisweet chocolate squares

To prepare crust: Lightly spray a 10-inch pie plate (preferably glass) with cooking spray. (A 10-inch springform pan with removable bottom will be fine, too.) Combine 3 cups of crushed cookie crumbs with the melted butter and press into bottom and sides of pie plate to form the crust. Place in freezer until firm, at least 1 hour.

To prepare filling: Create your first layer by placing the slightly soft coffee ice cream into a mixer fitted with a dough hook and mix until smooth, but not runny. Or mix by hand until the ice cream is the consistency of a very thick milkshake.

Remove crust from freezer and spread the ice cream onto the crust. Take remaining 1 cup cookie crumbs and combine with the crushed toffee. Reserve a handful for later and spread remaining mix on top of the coffee ice cream. Place pie back into freezer until very firm, at least 1 hour. Repeat with vanilla ice cream and place back into the freezer again until very firm, at least 1 hour.

To prepare the chocolate ganache topping: Heat the heavy cream until just boiling and add semisweet chocolate. Remove from heat. Let stand 2 minutes, then stir until smooth. Take pie from freezer and spread ganache over ice cream. Sprinkle your reserved handful of cookie and toffee mixture around the rim of pie. Place pie into freezer for 2 hours before serving. Remove pie from freezer 10 minutes before slicing to serve.

Serves 8 to 10

Strawberry-Champagne Tart

The airy white cake bottom hints of original strawberry shortcake roots, but this dish is much more sophisticated. With the effervescence of champagne encapsulated in a light, creamy tart and accents of strawberry slices, this dessert is simply pretty. Serving fresh is critical here, as after a day the strawberries start to fade and begin to lose their flavor.

cake:
    8 ounces sour cream
    ½ cup milk
    2¾ cups cake flour
    2 teaspoons baking powder
    ½ teaspoon salt
    8 tablespoons (1 stick) unsalted butter, room temperature
    2 cups sugar
    4 eggs
    1 teaspoon pure vanilla extract
    1 teaspoon pure almond extract

tart:
    3 pints fresh strawberries, sliced in half vertically
    1 cup plus ½ cup medium quality champagne, such as Korbel
    ½ cup granulated sugar
    2 teaspoons pure vanilla extract
    ½ lemon, juiced
    ¼ ounce gelatin
    4 egg yolks
    1½ cups heavy whipping cream
    ½ cup powdered sugar

strawberry sauce:
    1½ pounds ripe strawberries
    1 tablespoon cornstarch
    ⅓ cup, plus 1 teaspoon granulated sugar

    Crème Anglaise (recipe page 111)

To prepare cake: Preheat oven to 325°. Grease and flour a 9 x 13-inch pan. Combine sour cream and milk; set aside. In a separate bowl combine flour, baking powder, and salt; set aside. Cream butter and sugar until thick and light. Add eggs one at a time, mixing thoroughly after each. Alternately add flour mixture, then sour cream–milk mixture in three additions, beginning and ending with flour mixture. Stir in vanilla and almond extracts. Pour batter into prepared pan and bake for 40 to 45 minutes, until a toothpick inserted into center of cake comes out clean. Let cool in pan for 10 minutes before removing to wire racks. Cool completely before slicing or frosting.

To prepare tart: Grease eight individual 4-inch free-standing ring molds or a 9-inch springform pan with cooking spray. For the ring molds, place a 1-inch slice of cake on the bottom. Line rims of molds with the cut sides of strawberries against the metal.

For the springform pan, piece 1-inch slices of cake on the bottom, covering all metal. Line sides with the cut sides of strawberries against the metal. Tightly pack four or five whole strawberries together in the center of pan, on top of cake; this will make for a pretty cut when you slice the tart.

Combine the 1 cup of champagne, sugar, vanilla, and lemon juice; bring to a boil. Mix gelatin in the remaining ½ cup of champagne and set aside to soften. Temper egg yolks into champagne–lemon juice mixture and cook over medium heat, stirring constantly until thickened. Remove from heat and stir in softened gelatin mixture until dissolved. Let cool to lukewarm.

With an electric mixer or by hand with a wire whisk, whip heavy cream and powdered sugar until soft peaks form. Fold whipped cream into champagne mixture; mix thoroughly. Carefully pour mixture into prepared ring molds or pan and refrigerate for at least 3 hours.

To prepare strawberry sauce: Slice off tops of strawberries and puree berries in a blender or food processor. Strain through a fine mesh strainer. Measure and add water (if necessary) to make 2 cups of juice. Combine strawberry juice and cornstarch in a saucepan and stir over medium heat until combined. Add sugar. Cook over medium heat until sugar is dissolved and sauce thickens; simmer for 3 to 5 minutes. Let cool. You may need to thin sauce with water; if it is the consistency of jam it is too thick. Ideally you should be able to pour it with ease. Refrigerate before serving.

Serve tart chilled with strawberry sauce and Crème Anglaise drizzled decoratively over individual servings.

Serves 8

Coconut Almond Tart

An old favorite in the restaurant, this is always featured on the dessert cart. Inspired by the Almond Joy candy bar, it is a delectable combination of dark chocolate and coconut combined in a toasted almond crust.

crust:
> 1½ cups toasted almonds
> ¼ cup lightly packed brown sugar
> 4 tablespoons (½ stick) unsalted butter, melted

filling:
> ½ cup canned coconut cream (such as Coco López)
> 3 ounces white chocolate, chopped
> ¼ cup sour cream
> 4 tablespoons (½ stick) unsalted butter, cut into pieces, room temperature
> 1¼ cups shredded sweetened coconut, lightly packed

topping:
> ¼ cup heavy whipping cream
> 3 tablespoons unsalted butter
> 2 tablespoons light corn syrup
> 4 ounces bittersweet chocolate, chopped
> 2 ounces white chocolate, chopped and melted in double boiler

To prepare crust: Preheat oven to 350°. Coarsely chop almonds in a food processor or blender. Add sugar and melted butter. Process the mixture until finely chopped. Using plastic wrap as an aid, press mixture into the bottom and along the sides of a 9-inch tart pan with a removable bottom. Bake 10 minutes. Remove the pan from the oven and let it cool.

To prepare filling: Bring coconut cream to boil in a heavy saucepan. Reduce heat to low. Add white chocolate and stir until it is melted. Pour mixture into a medium bowl. Whisk in sour cream. Add butter and whisk until it melts into batter and the batter is a smooth consistency. Stir in shredded coconut. Chill until filling is very cold, but not set, about 1 hour. Spoon filling into crust, smooth top. Chill until set.

To prepare topping: In a heavy saucepan, combine whipping cream, butter, and corn syrup and bring to a low boil, stirring frequently. Reduce heat to low. Add bittersweet chocolate and stir until melted. Pour over tart, covering filling. Spread topping with back of spoon to cover evenly. Spoon melted white chocolate into pastry bag fitted with small tip. Pipe in parallel vertical lines over topping, spacing evenly. With a skewer or toothpick drag the lines to form a decorative pattern in the chocolate. Chill and serve.

Serves 12

Huckleberry Swirl Cheesecake

The Native Americans considered tiny, tart huckleberries an important food source, drink base, and material for dyes. In this dish they add a wonderful spin of purple color to this ultracreamy cheesecake. You can substitute blackberry or raspberry preserves if huckleberry preserves are not available.

2½ cups crushed graham crackers
½ teaspoon ground cinnamon
4 tablespoons (½ stick) butter, melted
2 pounds cream cheese, room temperature
1 cup sugar
4 eggs
Zest of 1 lemon
1 teaspoon pure vanilla extract
¼ teaspoon pure lemon extract
1 cup huckleberry preserves

Preheat oven to 325°. Lightly spray a 9-inch springform pan with cooking spray. Combine graham crackers, cinnamon, and melted butter. Press the graham cracker mixture on the bottom and up the sides of the springform pan. Bake for 6 minutes. Remove from oven and let cool. Wrap the outside bottom and sides of the pan with two layers of heavy aluminum foil and set aside.

Beat the cream cheese in an electric mixer or stir with a wooden spoon until smooth, frequently scraping down the sides of the bowl with a rubber spatula. Add sugar ¼ cup at a time and mix until very smooth again. Add eggs one at a time, scraping down the sides of the bowl after each addition. Add lemon zest and extracts.

Remove ¾ cup of cream cheese mixture to a separate bowl and add huckleberry preserves; mix until you have a smooth batter. Carefully pour remaining cream cheese mixture into the cooled crust. For a decorative touch, place huckleberry batter into a pastry bag fitted with a large tip; pipe intermittent dots of huckleberry batter into the plain batter. Take a sharp knife; carefully swirl dots in a crisscross motion, without scraping the bottom or sides of crust.

Place foil-wrapped pan in a larger pan and fill with hot water about halfway up the sides of pan. Bake for 60 minutes. Turn off oven and let the cheesecake cool in the oven with the door open for another 60 minutes. This will finish cooking the cheesecake slowly and prevent the top from splitting. Remove the springform pan from the water bath and place on wire rack to cool, then refrigerate overnight. Remove sides of springform pan to serve.

Serves 8

Lemon Pudding Cake
with Dried Cherry Compote

This light, airy dessert is fanciful and tangy. With its old-fashioned lemon flavor and syrupy-sweet cherry sauce, this is the perfect finish to a heavy meal.

2 tablespoons plus 1 teaspoon all-purpose flour
⅔ cup sugar
¼ teaspoon salt
2 tablespoons finely grated lemon zest
3 large eggs, separated, at room temperature
1¼ cups buttermilk
¼ cup freshly squeezed lemon juice

Preheat oven to 325°. Generously grease bottom and sides of 6 (4-ounce) ramekins or foil cups with butter. Coat with sugar (as you would with flour), and tap out excess.

In a large bowl, combine flour, sugar, salt, and lemon zest with a whisk. In a separate bowl whisk together egg yolks, buttermilk, and lemon juice until well blended. Pour liquid ingredients into dry ingredients and mix thoroughly. Set aside.

With an electric mixer, whip egg whites on medium speed until soft peaks form. Fold whites into batter in three additions. Using ladle, fill prepared cups almost to the top. Place cups in a baking dish. Pour hot water into pan to cover three-quarters of the way up the cups. Bake puddings for 15 minutes. Turn the pan around and bake for another 15 minutes, until pudding has risen and is firm to the touch. Remove cups from water bath and place on rack to cool slightly before serving. Serve with a Dried Cherry Compote.

Dried Cherry Compote:
6 ounces dried cherries
⅓ cup real maple syrup
¼ cup apple cider
¼ cup sugar
1 tablespoon pure vanilla extract

In a medium saucepan, combine cherries, maple syrup, apple cider, sugar, and vanilla.

Bring to a boil, stirring to dissolve sugar. Reduce heat and simmer about 10 minutes, until cherries have absorbed liquid and puffed up. Let cool. Store compote in an airtight container in refrigerator for up to a week.

Serves 6

Orange Blossom Brownies

The addition of orange zest in this recipe gives these decadent chocolate brownies a delicate balance of flavor that makes them appropriate at the most formal table or at a backyard barbecue.

6 eggs
3 cups sugar
1 cup canola oil
2 cups all-purpose flour, sifted
1 cup cocoa
1 teaspoon salt
½ cup walnuts or pecans (optional)
2 teaspoons pure vanilla extract
2 tablespoons freshly grated orange zest

Preheat oven to 350°. Beat eggs, add sugar and oil. Add flour, cocoa, and salt. Add nuts if using, vanilla, and orange zest. Mix only to combine, batter should still be lumpy. Turn batter into two greased 8 x 8-inch baking dishes or one 9 x 13-inch baking dish. Bake 40 to 45 minutes. Leave in pan to cool. Can be frosted or served plain.

frosting:
4 cups powdered sugar
4 heaping tablespoons cocoa
⅓ cup evaporated milk
4 tablespoons (½ stick) butter, softened
1 teaspoon pure vanilla extract

Combine all ingredients and mix on low speed until smooth, adding extra milk if necessary to make the icing more spreadable.

Serves 12

Flaming Orange

(see photo page 87)

Served since the late 1970s, this dramatic dessert is an original recipe from Chef Larry Edwards. It is a creative combination of whimsy and wildness, the childhood experience of a Creamsicle partnered with fascination for fire. The result is a pleasing concoction that elevates ice cream to new heights. When preparing this flashy dessert it is essential that you use high quality ice cream; Chico uses Wilcoxsons.

8 large oranges
10 ounces bittersweet chocolate

filling:
    4 cups of high-quality vanilla ice cream
    ½ ounce of Grand Marnier
    ½ ounce Triple Sec
    ½ ounce vodka
    ½ cup sour cream
    1 ounce frozen orange juice concentrate, thawed

meringue topping:
    4 egg whites, room temperature
    ¼ teaspoon cream of tartar
    ¾ cups sugar
    ¼ teaspoon almond extract

8 ounces of 151 rum

To prepare oranges: Cut the tops and bottoms from the oranges, making the top cut a little wider than the bottom. Hollow out each orange by running a grapefruit spoon halfway between the skin and the pulp on the top. Repeat this step on the bottom of each orange, then carefully push out the pulp. The inside of the orange should be clean of any pulp.

Melt bittersweet chocolate in a double boiler. Replace a pulp-free slice of orange end on the bottom of orange shell, creating a plug for the hollow rind. Line the inside of the orange with the melted chocolate using a soup spoon to smear it until all the white is covered. Repeat with remaining 7 oranges. Place oranges in the freezer at least until chocolate has hardened.

To prepare filling: Let the ice cream get slightly soft and place in the bowl of an electric mixer fitted with a dough hook. If preparing by hand, mix with a stiff plastic spatula. Mix or stir ice cream until it is the consistency of a thick milkshake; add remaining filling ingredients. Mix thoroughly. Fill the chocolate-lined oranges evenly; be careful not to overflow them. Place oranges in freezer until hardened, about 1 hour.

To prepare meringue topping: Whip egg whites with cream of tartar until soft peaks form. Slowly add the sugar a little at a time until stiff peaks form; add almond extract. Using a pastry bag with a rosette tip, pipe domes of meringue on the frozen oranges and return them to freezer.

When ready to serve, remove oranges from freezer, let stand 15 minutes at room temperature. Warm eight heat-resistant plates in a 400-degree oven for about 5 minutes. Place oranges on plates; place the hot plate over a cool plate for guests and pour about 1 ounce of 151 rum over each orange. Serve tableside and carefully light with a match. Let the flame burn out entirely before eating, it browns the meringue while softening the chocolate and ice cream.

Serves 8

Grand Marnier Crème Brulee

The warmth of an after dinner drink is combined with the smooth, creamy delicacy of this traditional dessert.

2 cups heavy whipping cream
⅓ cup sugar
5 egg yolks, room temperature
½ tablespoon pure vanilla extract
¼ cup Grand Marnier, brandy, or other liqueur
6 teaspoons sugar

Preheat oven to 325°. Heat the cream and sugar in a heavy saucepan until just boiling. Slowly pour in the egg yolks while whisking. Add the vanilla and the Grand Marnier. Pour into 6 ramekins or small oven-safe bowls. Place in a 9 x 13-inch baking dish and fill with a hot water bath three-quarters of the way up the outside of the bowls. Bake in the oven for about 40 minutes, or until set; the brulee should not jiggle in the center. Remove from oven and let cool in the water bath. Refrigerate for at least 2 hours or up to two days covered with plastic wrap.

When ready to serve, sprinkle a teaspoon of sugar on top of each custard. With a small, handheld butane torch, caramelize the sugar until dark brown and bubbly. The result is a hot, delicate crust over a cool, creamy middle. (Handheld butane torches are available at most cooking shops.)

You can also caramelize the sugar in the oven by placing the custards under the broiler and watching carefully until the sugar is dark brown and bubbly; this will heat the bowl completely and result in a "soupy" texture. Either way, let the sugar harden before serving.

Serves 6

Entertaining
Chico Style

Chico is a gathering place. It is where friends and family relive old memories and create new experiences. Whether they come together for a casual barbecue, an extravagant picnic, or an elegant wine dinner, there is food for every occasion. The food is half the fun.

In this chapter we've provided you with three very different menus for large parties, Chico style. We hope you'll try them all, add a special personal touch, and make them your own. Enjoy!

Extravagant Picnic, serves 12

Wine Cellar Dinner, serves 16

Western Barbecue, serves 25

Extravagant Picnic
Serves 12

Gingham tablecloths and picnic baskets spread across a meadow overlooking the Paradise Valley's Absaroka Mountains is the best place for a picnic like this. Or, in the cool shade of hundred-year-old cottonwood trees by the Yellowstone River isn't bad. By a waterfall after a picturesque hayride is just right, too. The venue is your choice, but the key is not to skimp on luxury or taste just because you are outside. Enjoying fine food in good company calls for champagne to set the tone of a festive and elegant meal; a sip of whimsical dessert wine seals the deal.

Menu
Mediterranean Olives
Paté
Lobster Salad
Capri Sandwiches
Chilled Herb-Roasted Chicken
Lemon Pound Cake with Lemon Verbena
Fresh Berry Medley
Coconut Macaroons
1 gallon sparkling water
2 bottles champagne, such as Veuve Cliquot Brut Rose
2 bottles of Steele's Late Harvest Chardonnay, 1991

Tools of the Trade
Large wicker basket
2 large tablecloths or blankets
12 Linen napkins
Flatware
Plates
Large serving platter
Serving tray for pate, olives and sandwiches
Serving spoons for Lobster salad and chicken
Corkscrew
Sharp knife
Light cutting board
Salt and pepper
Disposable towelettes
Garbage bags
Cooler with ice
Citronella candles
Matches
Flashlight
Insect repellent
Portable CD player

Mediterranean Olives

1 red bell pepper
5 cloves garlic
1 cup, plus 1 tablespoon extra virgin olive oil
4 ounces Kalamata olives, drained (whole or pitted)
4 ounces green Spanish olives, drained (whole or pitted)
1 bay leaf
1 quart-sized mason jar
French bread

Roast whole red bell pepper over an open flame on a gas burning stovetop or grill; remove from flame when skin is mostly blackened and immerse in an ice bath to remove skin easily. Pepper can also be roasted in the oven at 400° for 10 to 20 minutes. Seed and slice into 1-inch-wide strips. Set aside.

Preheat oven to 400°. Toss garlic cloves in 1 tablespoon olive oil and place in a baking dish. Roast in the oven for 10 minutes. Combine roasted garlic with roasted pepper. Add olives, 1 cup oil, and bay leaf; toss until well coated. Place olive mixture in mason jar and marinate for 24 hours in refrigerator; will keep up to two weeks. Serve in jar or decorative bowl with French bread to soak up olive oil as an appetizer.

Paté

6 to 8 ounces of high quality paté (found in most specialty food stores)
1 package Carr's water table crackers or your favorite cracker

Spread paté generously on crackers and enjoy.

Lobster Salad

1¾ cups mayonnaise
¾ cup chili sauce (Del Monte)
3 tablespoons finely chopped parsley
3 tablespoons fresh lemon juice
3 teaspoons drained bottle horseradish
2 teaspoons Worcestershire sauce
Fine sea salt and pepper to taste
1½ cups chopped and drained canned hearts of palm
3 tablespoons capers to garnish (optional)
1 pound fresh lobster meat, cut into bite-size chunks
1 bunch watercress, coarse stems discarded
2 cucumbers, seeded and sliced
6 pita breads, sliced into triangles

In a bowl whisk mayonnaise, chili sauce, parsley, lemon juice, horseradish, Worcestershire sauce, salt, and pepper together. Fold in hearts of palm, optional capers, and lobster. Combine the mixture gently but thoroughly.

Transfer the lobster salad to a chilled platter lined with watercress and serve it with the cucumber slices and pita triangles. The lobster salad may be prepared one day in advance and kept covered in the refrigerator.

Capri Sandwiches

Herb Focaccia:

7 cups all-purpose flour
2½ to 3 cups water (approximately 105°)
1 tablespoon Italian seasoning
2 tablespoons fresh thyme leaves
3½ tablespoons sea salt, divided
4 teaspoons instant yeast
¼ cup, plus 3 tablespoons extra virgin olive oil
¼ cup cornmeal
1 cup fresh grated Parmesan cheese

1 cup Basil Oil (recipe page 110)
1½ pounds fresh mozzarella, sliced
6 to 8 Roma tomatoes, sliced
3 pounds shaved prosciutto
Sea salt and black pepper to taste

To prepare Herb Focaccia: Mix flour, warm water, Italian seasoning, fresh thyme, 2½ tablespoons sea salt, yeast, and ¼ cup olive oil in a mixing bowl. Knead with hands until a soft, semi-sticky dough forms. Add more water if dough seems dry. Grease a clean mixing bowl with 1 tablespoon olive oil; transfer dough and cover with plastic wrap. Allow dough to rise until it doubles in size (about 45 minutes).

Prepare a 12 x 16-inch baking sheet or 2 (9 x 13-inch) baking dishes by greasing with 1 tablespoon olive oil and sprinkling lightly with cornmeal. Punch dough down flat and gently work it into a rectangular piece(s), spread evenly onto oiled pan(s); cover with plastic wrap and let rise until doubled again (about 1 hour).

Preheat oven to 400°. When dough has risen, dimple the dough with fingers, brush with 1 tablespoon olive oil, and sprinkle with remaining tablespoon sea salt or to taste. Sprinkle with grated Parmesan cheese. Bake for 15 to 20 minutes or until golden brown.

Let cool completely. Cut into 12 (4-inch-square) pieces, then slice through the center of each piece with a bread knife to yield two thinner squares for sandwiches.

Drizzle focaccia slices with Basil Oil and layer with cheese, tomatoes, prosciutto, and salt and pepper to taste; wrap in plastic wrap until ready to serve.

Chilled Herb-Roasted Chicken

2 tablespoons kosher salt
Black pepper to taste
4 cloves garlic, sliced
1 cup fresh whole thyme leaves
1 cup fresh whole sage leaves
1 cup chopped fresh basil
1 cup fresh whole oregano leaves
4 cups, plus 4 tablespoons olive oil
8 lemons
12 large chickens, cut into quarters

In a bowl, combine salt, pepper, garlic, herbs. In a large pan, heat 4 cups olive oil until almost smoking; pour over herbs. Stir until combined and let sit for 1 minute. Juice lemons and pour into herb oil. Remove any remaining seeds from lemon rinds, and add rinds to herb oil. Place chicken in herb oil; marinate in the refrigerator for at least 3 hours.

Preheat oven to 350°. Heat a large pan and add 4 tablespoons fresh olive oil and marinated chicken. Fry until skin on all pieces is golden, turning often. Place chicken in two baking dishes and bake for 15 to 20 minutes. Test the thickest piece for doneness. Chill until ready to serve.

Lemon Pound Cake with Lemon Verbena

½ pound (2 sticks) unsalted butter, room temperature
3 cups sugar
6 eggs, room temperature
3 tablespoons chopped fresh lemon verbena leaves (can substitute optimally with hard-to-find key lime zest, finely grated, or zest of a regular lime, finely grated)
1 tablespoon finely grated lemon zest
2 tablespoons fresh lemon juice
2 tablespoons milk
3 cups cake flour, sifted
½ teaspoon baking powder
1 cup sour cream
1 teaspoon pure vanilla extract

Preheat oven to 300°. Grease and flour 2 (6-inch) bread pans. Cream butter and sugar together until light and fluffy. Add eggs, two at a time, beating thoroughly after each addition. Add the lemon verbena, lemon zest, lemon juice, and milk.

Sift the cake flour and baking powder together; then add these dry ingredients to butter mixture, alternating with sour cream. Do this in four additions, beginning and ending with dry ingredients. Add vanilla and mix, being careful not to overmix.

Fill bread pans with cake batter and smooth tops. Bake for 1 hour and 15 to 20 minutes, until a toothpick inserted in the center comes out clean. Cool in pan 10 minutes, then invert on a rack to finish cooling. Tightly wrap in plastic wrap and refrigerate overnight.

Fresh Berry Medley

1 pint fresh raspberries
1 pint fresh blackberries
1 pint fresh blueberries
¼ cup chopped fresh mint leaves
Juice of ½ lemon

Combine berries, mint, and lemon juice; toss and serve.

Coconut Macaroons

4 egg whites
¼ teaspoon salt
¾ cup sugar
¾ cup powdered sugar
1 teaspoon pure vanilla extract
1½ cups shredded sweetened coconut
½ cup bittersweet chocolate

Preheat oven to 325°. Grease baking sheets or line with parchment paper. In an electric mixer using the whisk attachment, or by hand, beat egg whites and salt on high speed until frothy. Combine the sugars in a separate bowl and gradually add to the egg whites. Add the vanilla and continue to beat on high speed or mix rigorously until stiff. Carefully fold in coconut on low speed or by hand with a rubber spatula. With a melon ball scoop or teaspoon, scoop on to prepared baking sheets. Bake for 15 minutes. Cool on a wire rack. Once the cookies have cooled, melt the chocolate in the microwave or in a double boiler. Drizzle cookies with the melted chocolate.

Yields 2 dozen cookies

Chico for All Seasons

At Chico, appreciating Montana's beauty and culture becomes accessible to anyone. Use the resort as a base to enjoy unspoiled Paradise Valley and the surrounding wonders.

During summer and fall there is the world famous Yellowstone River, just minutes away from Chico. Ribboning through the center of the valley, this river offers more than fifty miles of unparalleled fishing, whitewater rafting, and toe-dipping on hot summer days.

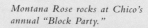

Montana Rose rocks at Chico's annual "Block Party."

Horseback riding, hayrides, and hundreds of miles of hiking trails are just out the lodge's front door. Explore Yellowstone National Park, just thirty-five miles away. You'll see wildlife and geysers and fantastic wilderness, but still be able to come "home" to Chico.

In the snowy winter and spring months it's tempting to cozy up to the wood burning stove in the lobby with a good book, but make time for outdoor adventures, too. Dog sledding, cross-country skiing, sledding, and visits into Yellowstone National Park are wonderful ways to explore the area. Afterward you can warm up chilled bones and catch snowflakes on your tongue in the soothing hot springs pools.

If all that sounds too strenuous, then indulge in a massage at Chico Day Spa or really spoil yourself with an extensive day of beauty: facials, body scrubs, mud wraps, and more. But when you are finished, don't forget to put on your dancing shoes for weekend music in the saloon. Or catch one of the Summer Series events, from a Shakespearean play on the lawn to an orchestra performance by twilight.

Each year Chico hosts a variety of events for guests and the public, such as the Chico Mystery Weekends, the summer Golf Tournament, and the annual Skydivers' Weekend. Many guests return year after year for family holidays, vacations, reunions, weddings, or business meetings. Chico is a destination for all seasons.

Dog sledding is just one of many seasonal adventures offered at Chico.

Judith Strom photo

Wine Cellar Dinner

Serves 16

Behind the historic main lodge is a quaint stone building that houses Chico's wine cellar and a small private dining room. The building once housed the inn's original generator. Today it holds a fifteen-foot-long harvest table and echoes of glasses chinking in the toasts that have been given here during countless celebrations. Candlelight and privacy make for an atmosphere that is rustic and intimate; secret and delightful. This menu was created to be served on large platters family-style for bountiful sharing.

Menu

Pine Nut Crusted Halibut Appetizer
Garden Green Salad with Orange Vinaigrette
Green Beans with Toasted Almonds
Butternut Squash and Pine Nuts
Sautéed Lentils
Orange-Glazed Quail with Pecan Cornbread Stuffing
Grilled Venison Loin
New York Cheesecake

Wine Suggestions

Appetizer course: Luna Vineyard's Pinot Grigio adds a light, apple complement to the fruity halibut.

Salad course: Steele Chardonnay, offers a palate-cleansing, cuvée-style wine.

Main course: Archery Summit Pinot Noir and Zenato Amarone, two very different reds from the Northwest and Italy respectively that match the earthy richness of the wild game offerings for this menu.

Dessert course: Michaele Chiarlo Nivole, a deeply layered dessert wine from an Italian master.

Pine Nut Crusted
Halibut Appetizer

Use the entrée version of this recipe (page 52),
but begin with 4 (8-ounce) halibut fillets, rather
than the slightly smaller fillets suggested for
entrées. (The remaining ingredients are
sufficient to prepare the extra portions of fillet.)
The only change in halibut preparation is to
cut each 8-ounce fillet into 4 small portions,
approximately 2 ounces each. This will allow
for 16 appetizer-size pieces. Continue to follow
the entrée version of the recipe until the end.
Since this is the appetizer course, it is the only
item that should be served on individual plates.
Present the halibut on a pool of Port Wine
Butter Sauce (recipe page 113), topped with the
fresh Mango Salsa (recipe page 113).

Garden Green Salad with
Orange Vinaigrette

2 pounds mixed greens
2 cups Orange–Ginger Vinaigrette (recipe page 37)
1 red onion, thinly sliced
1/4 pound Maytag blue cheese, crumbled
1/4 pound toasted walnuts, rough chopped

Just before serving time, toss greens in a large
bowl. Begin with half the dressing and add
more as needed so that you do not overdress.
Once greens are tossed and lightly coated with
dressing, top with onion, cheese, and walnuts.

Green Beans
with Toasted Almonds

8 tablespoons (1 stick) unsalted butter
2 cloves garlic, sliced
3 pounds fresh green beans, trimmed
1 large sweet onion, sliced
Juice of 1 lemon
1/2 cup toasted almonds
Salt and pepper to taste

Preheat sauté pan. Add butter, garlic, green
beans, and onion. Stir until desired doneness;
add lemon juice, salt and pepper to taste, and
toasted almonds. Stir and serve.

Butternut Squash
and Pine Nuts

4 pounds butternut squash, seeded, cut in half, and
    sliced
8 tablespoons (1 stick) butter
1/4 cup brown sugar
1/4 cup toasted pine nuts
1/4 cup chopped parsley

Preheat oven to 400°. Steam squash for
approximately 20 minutes until skin is pierced
easily with a knife point. Arrange squash slices
on a baking sheet face up. In a small saucepan,
melt butter and brown sugar together, drizzle
over squash. Sprinkle with nuts and parsley.
Bake for 20 minutes. It is done when it is nice
and brown.

Sautéed Lentils

8 cups dried lentils
¼ cup canola or corn oil
¼ cup bacon fat
1 cup diced celery
1 large red onion, diced
1 clove garlic, diced
1 red bell pepper, diced
4 cups Chicken Stock (recipe page 111)

In a large skillet, heat lentils on high heat with no oil until they start to brown and smoke. Add oil and bacon fat, stir until blended. Sauté for about 3 minutes; add celery, onion, garlic, and pepper. Sauté until vegetables are brown; add stock 1 cup at a time. Keep on high heat, stir until stock reduces. Beans should have a slight crunch to them.

Orange-Glazed Quail with Pecan Cornbread Stuffing

1 large yellow onion, diced
½ cup diced celery
8 strips of bacon, diced
½ cup dried cranberries (sweetened or
   unsweetened) or raisins
½ cup heavy whipping cream
½ cup sherry
½ cup Chicken Stock (recipe page 111)
1 teaspoon sage
1 teaspoon salt
1 teaspoon pepper
1 teaspoon poultry seasoning
1 (9 x 13-inch) baking dish of Maple Cornbread
   (recipe page 107)
½ cup toasted pecans
16 deboned quail
Salt, pepper, and paprika to taste
½ cup orange marmalade

Sauté onion, celery, and bacon on medium-high heat until brown. Add cranberries or raisins, cream, sherry, stock, and seasonings. Stir and reduce liquid by two-thirds. Mash cornbread and pecans in a bowl, pour in sauté mixture, and mash with a wooden spoon. Allow to cool.

Preheat oven to 450°. Use a tablespoon to shape stuffing into a ball, stuff into quail. Allow enough room to fold the legs over one another. Take a wooden toothpick and pierce through each leg to tuck neatly into the body. Sprinkle with salt, pepper, paprika, and bake for approximately 10 minutes until golden brown. Brush orange marmalade on skin and cook 5 minutes more to caramelize. Test that the stuffing is hot before removing; remove toothpick before serving.

Grilled Venison Loin

5 pounds venison tenderloin
3 cups red wine
½ cup fresh thyme
½ cup fresh savory
½ cup fresh oregano
2 tablespoons cracked black peppercorns
1 tablespoon sea salt
4 large shallots, rough chopped
2 tablespoons whole-grain Dijon mustard
¼ cup red wine vinegar

Cut venison into approximately 20 (4-ounce) steaks. Combine remaining ingredients in a large bowl and add steaks. Marinate in the refrigerator for at least 6 hours. Grill to rare or desired temperature:

Temperature Chart:	
Rare	1 to 3 minutes on each side
Medium rare	3 to 4 minutes on each side
Medium	5 to 6 minutes on each side
Medium well	7 to 10 minutes on each side

New York Cheesecake

crust:
- 1 tablespoon unsalted butter, softened
- ¼ cup graham cracker crumbs

topping:
- 1 pint sour cream
- ¼ cup sugar
- 1 tablespoon lemon juice
- ¼ teaspoon pure vanilla extract

cake:
- (all ingredients should be at room temperature)
- 1¾ cups sugar
- 3 tablespoons all-purpose flour
- 2½ pounds (40 ounces) cream cheese
- ½ teaspoon pure almond extract
- ½ teaspoon pure vanilla extract
- 5 large eggs
- 2 large egg yolks
- ½ cup heavy whipping cream

Fresh berries and lemon zest for garnish

To prepare the crust: Coat the bottom and sides of a 9-inch springform pan with butter. Sprinkle graham cracker crumbs in the pan; tilt and tap the pan to spread the crumbs evenly over the bottom and sides. Set aside.

To prepare the topping: Combine sour cream, sugar, lemon juice, and vanilla in a bowl; mix well. Refrigerate until ready to use.

To prepare the cake: Preheat oven to 500°. In a large mixing bowl, combine sugar and flour, mix well. With an electric mixer (and in a separate bowl) beat cream cheese until light and creamy, about 30 to 60 seconds. Scrape the sides of bowl and mixer attachment; gradually add and combine flour mixture until smooth, 1 to 2 minutes. Add almond and vanilla extracts, mix until combined. Adding eggs and yolks one at a time, mix until just incorporated, scraping the sides of the bowl and the mixer attachment after each addition. Add heavy whipping cream, mixing on low speed.

Pour and scrape batter into prepared springform pan and smooth the top. Bake for 15 minutes, then reduce the oven temperature to 200° and bake for 1 hour more. Turn the oven off and prop the oven door ajar (use the handle of a wooden spoon if necessary), and let the cake cool for 30 minutes in the oven. Remove from oven to cool on a rack; spread with sour cream topping and allow to cool completely. Refrigerate for at least 6 hours, preferably 24 hours. After 48 hours the cheese flavor is even more intense. Serve with fresh berries or a sprinkling of lemon zest on each slice.

Winning Wines

Chico's wine list was crafted to complement its classic cuisine as well as to appeal to the diverse clientele who walks through Chico's doors. From banker to rancher, from Europe to Livingston, there was a need to satisfy almost every palate of almost every guest. The goal is to offer an approachable, affordable, and extensive collection of wines. We want our guests to be as comfortable selecting wine as they are ordering from our menu; at Chico that means quality and diversity. The idea is to be able to find easy drinking favorites along with that aging Bordeaux or California cult classic tucked away for just the right customer.

Our list represents a wide variety of California and Northwest wines. The Italian and French offerings are extensive as well, laced with unusual jewels and hard-to-find vintages. The list also features larger format bottles from magnums of Silver Oak, Opus One, and Ornellaia to multiple bottle verticals of Beringer Private Reserve Cabernet, Italian Brunellos, and progressive years of Sassicaia. A further compliment to the cuisine is the breadth of the champagne and dessert wine collection.

As a result, the restaurant has received the coveted *Wine Spectator* magazine's "Award of Excellence" for four years since 1999. But more than acclaim, we've cultivated a loyal clientele who savors our program of food and wine. Careful planning and extensive staff training are all part of our wine program. Whether you select a familiar label or feel like trying something adventurous, our crew can pair wines to match your personal taste and meal.

Western Barbecue

Serves 25

For a large gathering outside in the summer, this menu of meaty pork ribs and tender chicken makes for an easy, memorable meal to share with a large group. At Chico it is served on the front lawn, with the historic lodge and Emigrant Peak in the background. The summer sun hangs long and evening lingers until all this hearty food has dwindled.

Menu
St. Louis-Style Ribs
Montana Chicken
Corn on the Cob
Baked Beans
Cabbage and Jicama Slaw
Maple Cornbread
Huckleberry Cobbler
Montana microbrews (Headstrong Pale Ale and Moose Drool are local favorites at Chico.)
Shooting Star Sauvignon Blanc
Lemonade

St. Louis-Style Ribs

8 full racks of pork ribs (about 15 pounds)
3 cups barbecue seasoning, such as Lawry's
1 gallon barbecue sauce

Coat ribs with barbecue seasoning. Grill for 3 minutes on each side. Remove from grill and let cool. When cool enough to cut, slice racks into 2-piece riblets.

Preheat oven to 350°. Arrange riblets in an orderly fashion in 2 (9 x 13-inch) baking dishes, and bake for 2½ to 3 hours. Meat should be tender and juicy. Brush generously with barbecue sauce and return to oven for 20 minutes. The ribs should have a nice caramelized glaze when done. Remaining barbecue sauce can be warmed and served on the side.

Montana Chicken

15 pounds chicken (leg, thigh, wing, and breast)
2 cups barbecue seasoning

Preheat oven to 450°. Briefly sear each piece of chicken on a grill to mark the skin, dusting each side with barbecue seasoning. Place seared chicken pieces in 2 (9 x 13-inch) baking dishes, generously sprinkling more barbecue seasoning until coated. Bake for 30 to 45 minutes; skin should be crispy and golden to dark in color.

Corn on the Cob

30 ears of corn
½ pound (2 sticks) salted butter

Husk corn and break each ear in half. Place in a large stockpot and cover with water; cook 20 minutes. Drain water, but leave corn in pot. Add butter and toss corn in the melted butter. Transfer to a platter and cover with foil until ready to serve.

Baked Beans

2 (10-pound) cans of baked beans
½ pound bacon, diced
2 large red onions, diced
1 pound (4 sticks) salted butter
Salt and pepper to taste

Pour canned beans into a large pot and begin a slow warm up on medium heat. Sauté bacon in another pan on high heat until just brown. Add onions, cook until translucent. Add bacon, onions, and butter to beans. Stir gently, adding salt and pepper to taste. Heat thoroughly and serve.

Cabbage and Jicama Slaw

3 large heads purple cabbage, julienned
2 large heads green cabbage, julienned
3 jicama roots, peeled and julienned
1 cup balsamic vinegar
1 cup extra virgin olive oil
½ cup fennel seeds
Salt and pepper to taste

Combine all ingredients and mix thoroughly. Serve chilled.

Maple Cornbread

1 cup milk
1 cup buttermilk
4 eggs
1½ cups vegetable oil
½ tablespoon maple extract
1½ cups cornmeal
3 cups bread flour
1 tablespoon salt
1 tablespoon baking powder

Preheat oven to 350°. Spray a 9 x 13-inch baking dish with cooking spray. Combine milk, buttermilk, eggs, oil, and maple extract in a mixing bowl and whisk to combine. Sift together cornmeal, flour, salt, and baking powder, and add to batter. Mix only enough to combine; be careful not to overmix. Pour batter into prepared baking dish, and bake for 30 minutes, or until golden and set. Serve with Honey Butter.

Honey Butter:
½ pound (2 sticks) butter, softened
¼ cup honey

Whip butter and honey together in a mixer or by hand with a wooden spoon until creamy. Serve at room temperature.

Huckleberry Cobbler

Shortbread Crust:
12 tablespoons (1½ sticks) unsalted butter, cold and cut into cubes
¾ cup powdered sugar
1½ cups all-purpose flour
½ teaspoon salt

Sweet Biscuit Topping:
3 cups all-purpose flour
½ teaspoon salt
2 teaspoons baking powder
4 tablespoons (½ stick) unsalted butter, cold and cut into cubes
1 cup sugar
1½ cups heavy whipping cream

Fresh Huckleberry Mix:
12 cups fresh huckleberries (you can substitute any kind of fresh berry or use thawed frozen berries if fresh are not available)
1 cup flour
1 cup sugar
2 tablespoons grated lemon peel

To prepare Shortbread Crust: Preheat oven to 350°. Combine all ingredients and mix by hand or in an electric mixer until a dough ball forms. Spread evenly over the bottom of a 9 x 13-inch glass baking dish. Bake until lightly browned (about 15 minutes).

To prepare Sweet Biscuit Topping: Combine the flour, salt, and baking powder; mix well. Add cold butter and whisk by hand or with an electric mixer until a course mixture forms. Add sugar and mix until incorporated. Slowly add cream and mix until a dough forms. Set aside.

To prepare Fresh Huckleberry Mix: Preheat oven to 350°. Lightly toss berries with the flour, sugar, and lemon peel. Pour berry mix into the pan over the baked Shortbread Crust. Distribute little pieces of the Sweet Biscuit Topping dough on top of berries. Bake for about 1½ hours, or until the topping is browned and the juice from the berries has thickened to a syrupy consistency. Allow to cool about 30 minutes. Serve warm.

Chef's Cupboard

This chapter is about the basics. The sauces can be used with the recipes in this book and with your other favorites. The stock preparations are tried and true. Though they may seem like a lot of extra work, when paired with fresh, quality ingredients, these are the recipes that set Chico's dining room apart.

Balsamic Vinegar Reduction Sauce

Basil Oil

Basil-Mint Jelly

Beef Stock

Chicken Stock

Crème Anglaise

Crostini

Dark Duck Stock

Fresh Citrus Vinaigrette

Garlic Butter

Hollandaise Sauce

Mango Salsa

Port Wine Butter Sauce

Port Wine Sauce

Shrimp Stock

Sundried Tomato Compound Butter

Veal Stock

Balsamic Vinegar Reduction Sauce

1 cup balsamic vinegar

In a saucepan reduce vinegar over medium heat until it forms a syrup (about 20 minutes). If it coats a spoon, the sauce is done.

Yields ¼ cup

Basil Oil

This is a versatile concoction; it can be used to toss pasta, for dipping French bread or brushed on Crostini (recipe page 112), as a base for salad dressing, or even as a marinade for fish and chicken.

1 cup fresh basil, packed without stems
½ cup grape seed oil (canola oil can be substituted)
12-inch piece of cheesecloth

Blanch basil in boiling water for 10 seconds. Shock in ice water. Pat dry with paper towels. It is important to dry the leaves thoroughly; water will make the oil separate. Combine basil and oil in a blender and blend for 30 seconds. Strain Basil Oil through cheesecloth, do not squeeze.

Yields ¼ to ½ cup

Basil-Mint Jelly

This delicate garnish for lamb and wild game was perfected by Chico's head banquet chef, Craig Flick, who borrowed the recipe from his mother, Virginia.

1½ cups fresh basil, packed, then rough chopped
2¼ cups water
3½ cups sugar
2 drops green food color
Juice of 1 lemon
1½ ounces of liquid pectin or 1 ounce of powdered pectin
3 tablespoons chopped fresh mint

In a saucepan, bring basil and water to a boil. Remove from heat and let stand for 10 minutes (this steeps the essence of the basil into the water). After 10 minutes, strain and save 1¾ cups of basil tea. Pour basil tea back into saucepan, add sugar, food color, and lemon juice. Bring the mixture to a boil, stirring constantly. Add pectin and return to a boil for 1 minute. Remove the pan from heat and add mint. Let the jelly set up overnight on the stovetop. In the morning, refrigerate jelly in small serving containers or classic jelly jars.

Yields 4 cups

Beef Stock

5 pounds beef bones (also called soup bones)
5 ounces tomato paste
4 large carrots, peeled, rough chopped
1 head celery, rough chopped
2 large white onions, rough chopped
1 bunch parsley or stems, rough chopped
3 bay leaves
1 tablespoon black peppercorns
2 tablespoons kosher salt
1 cup red wine

Preheat oven to 400°. Roast bones on a baking sheet until partially brown. Thin tomato paste with a little water and brush on bones. Continue to roast until bones are dark brown but not burnt. Place bones and remaining ingredients in a large (3-gallon) stockpot. Fill with cold water just over the top of ingredients. Simmer over medium heat for 6 to 12 hours; skim fat off
top and strain. Stock keeps up to 3 days in refrigerator; if not used by then it should be frozen or discarded.

Yields 4 quarts

Chicken Stock

1 small whole chicken (3 pounds)
1 whole duck (4 to 5 pounds)
3 large carrots, peeled, rough chopped
6 stalks celery, rough chopped
2 large white onions, rough chopped
4 cloves garlic, rough chopped
1 bunch parsley or stems, rough chopped
3 bay leaves
1 tablespoon black peppercorns
2 tablespoons kosher salt

Place chicken and duck with organs and necks in a large (3-gallon) stockpot; add other ingredients. Fill with cold water just over the top of ingredients. Simmer over medium heat for 6 to 12 hours; skim fat off top and strain. Stock keeps up to 3 days in refrigerator; if not used by then it should be frozen or discarded.

Yields 6 quarts

Crème Anglaise

3 egg yolks
⅓ cup, plus 2 tablespoons sugar
1 cup half-and-half
1 teaspoon pure vanilla extract

Combine egg yolks and sugar, whip until light and fluffy. In a saucepan, bring half-and-half to a slight boil, gently fold in yolk mixture. Place on a double boiler over simmering water until the mixture reaches between 180° to 190°, not above. Sauce is done when it coats the back of a spoon. Stir in vanilla extract, transfer to a cool bowl or small pitcher. Let cool to room temperature and refrigerate until ready to serve.

Yields 1 cup

Crostini

1 loaf Heirloom Bread (recipe page 19),
   ½-inch thick slices
¼ cup extra virgin olive oil

Preheat oven to 400°. Brush bread slices with olive oil on both sides. Bake for 10 to 15 minutes in the oven; reserve until later or serve immediately.

Dark Duck Stock

1 whole duck (at least 5 pounds)
3 large carrots, peeled, rough chopped
6 stalks celery, rough chopped
1 large yellow onion, rough chopped
4 cloves garlic, rough chopped
1 bunch parsley, rough chopped
2 bay leaves
1 tablespoon black peppercorns
1 tablespoon kosher salt

In a large (3-gallon) stockpot, combine duck (including organs and neck) with remaining ingredients. Fill with cold water just over the top of ingredients. Bring to a boil and let simmer for 6 to 8 hours; skim fat off top and strain. Stock keeps up to 3 days in refrigerator; if not used by then it should be frozen or discarded.

Yields 1½ gallons

Fresh Citrus Vinaigrette

1 grapefruit
1 orange
1 lemon
1 lime
1 teaspoon Dijon mustard
¼ cup extra virgin olive oil
1 teaspoon sugar
½ teaspoon salt

Juice all fruits and combine with remaining ingredients in a blender, or whisk by hand, until emulsified. Chill.

Yields 2 cups

Garlic Butter

½ pound (2 sticks) unsalted butter, softened
1 teaspoon dry mustard
1 teaspoon Worcestershire sauce
1 tablespoon minced garlic
½ teaspoon granulated onion

Mix all ingredients thoroughly with an electric mixer or by hand using a wooden spoon. While butter is soft, roll it into a 1-inch by 6-inch log in plastic wrap and refrigerate.

Hollandaise Sauce

½ pound (2 sticks) and 2 tablespoons unsalted butter
3 egg yolks, room temperature
2 tablespoons white wine
Juice of 1 lemon
1 teaspoon salt
½ teaspoon cayenne pepper

Melt butter over medium heat and skim foam off top with a large spoon to prepare clarified butter. Heat clarified butter to 95°. In a separate saucepan, add egg yolks and white wine, whisk over medium heat until the mixture thickens (about 3 minutes). Remove mixture from heat and slowly drizzle 95° butter into the pan, constantly stirring. (The temperature of the butter is crucial, measure it with a thermometer.) Once all butter has been incorporated, add remaining ingredients while continuing to stir.

Yields about 1 cup

Mango Salsa

1 mango, seeded, peeled, and diced
½ small red onion, diced
½ red bell pepper, diced
½ cup chopped chives
3 tablespoons raspberry vinegar
2 tablespoons honey
2 tablespoons chopped cilantro

Mix all ingredients together in a bowl and refrigerate until needed.

Yields 2 cups

Port Wine Butter Sauce

2 cups port wine
½ cup heavy whipping cream
8 tablespoons (1 stick) butter

This sauce cannot be reheated or chilled, so prepare it while the main course is in the oven or just before serving. Reduce port over medium heat until it forms a syrup (about 20 minutes). If it coats a spoon, it is ready. Add cream, reduce until thick. Remove from heat and add butter, stirring constantly until melted and smooth. Use immediately.

Yields 2 cups

Port Wine Sauce

1½ cups port wine
1 cup sweet vermouth
¼ cup sugar

Combine ingredients in a small saucepan. Reduce over medium heat until the mixture forms a syrup (about 30 minutes). If it coats a spoon, the sauce is done.

Shrimp Stock

2 tablespoons vegetable oil
2 small onions, diced
2 small carrots, peeled and diced
2 celery stalks, diced
Uncooked reserved lobster and shrimp shells, well
    rinsed and drained
3 cups cold water
1 bay leaf
½ tablespoon lightly crushed black peppercorns
1 teaspoon Pernod or ¼ teaspoon fennel seeds

Heat oil in a stockpot over medium-high heat. Add onions, carrots, and celery, then lobster and shrimp shells; cook until bright pink and aromatic (about 15 minutes), stirring occasionally. Add cold water, bay leaf, crushed peppercorns, and Pernod or fennel seeds. Bring almost to a boil, reduce heat to medium-low and simmer partially covered for 20 minutes. Strain into a clean pot, pressing down on shells to extract all the liquid. Let cool uncovered, then refrigerate until ready to use. Stock keeps only 1 day in refrigerator; if not used by then it should be frozen or discarded.

Yields ½ gallon

Sundried Tomato Compound Butter

½ pound (2 sticks) unsalted butter, softened
4 tablespoons diced sundried tomatoes
2 tablespoons minced chives
1 tablespoon minced garlic
1 teaspoon powdered mustard
1 teaspoon Worcestershire sauce
1 teaspoon black pepper
½ cup white wine

Whip butter in a mixer until it doubles in size. Add remaining ingredients and mix for 3 minutes, scraping the side of the bowl to ensure it is thoroughly combined. Spoon the mixture into a pastry bag with a large star tip and pipe into 1-ounce patties (about the size of a tablespoon). Instead of a pastry bag, you may also use plastic wrap to shape the butter mixture into a 1-inch-thick log. For either method, refrigerate until butter is set, about 2 hours. If you choose to use plastic wrap, unwrap the chilled butter and slice into ½-inch pieces before serving.

Veal Stock

5 pounds veal bones (sliced shin bones used in
    Osso Bucco, knuckles, or veal shanks with meat)
5 ounces tomato paste
4 large carrots, peeled, rough chopped
1 head celery, rough chopped
2 large white onions, rough chopped
1 bunch parsley or stems, rough chopped
3 bay leaves
1 tablespoon black peppercorns
2 tablespoons kosher salt
1 cup red wine

Preheat oven to 400°. Roast bones on a baking sheet until partially brown. Thin tomato paste with a little water and brush on bones; roast until bones are dark brown but not burnt. Place remaining ingredients in a large (3-gallon) stockpot. Fill with cold water just over the top of ingredients. Simmer over medium heat for 6 to 12 hours; skim fat off top and strain. Stock keeps up to 3 days in refrigerator; if not used by then it should be frozen or discarded.

Yields 1½ gallons

Specialty Ingredient Sources

Broken Arrow Ranch, Inc.
A Texas Corporation
P.O. Box 530
Ingram, TX 78025
1–800–962–4263
www.brokenarrowranch.com
Restaurant quality wild game, from bison to duck to
   deer.

Game Sales International, Inc.
P.O. Box 7719
Loveland, CO 80537–0719
(970) 667–4090
1–800–729–2090
Wild game products.

High Altitude Cooking and Baking

All of the recipes in the book are regularly prepared at 5,300 feet; they have been tested at altitudes above 4,000 feet. Normally anything made above 3,000 feet is considered high altitude cooking. If you live at 3,000 feet or below, then you can expect minor adjustments when preparing these dishes. Essentially you are converting to "low altitude cooking," but this is a simple alteration. You will need to be most attentive to adjustments when baking: Beyond water or sauce coming to a boil faster at higher altitude, the other recipes remain the same. There are no hard and fast rules for altitude adjustments in cooking, but here are some suggestions to make your recipes more savory.

For cakes: This applies to the Chico Carrot Cake, Chocolate Roulade, Lemon Pudding Cake and the Strawberry–Champagne Tart. The trickiest and most appealing characteristic of a cake is its delicacy. Because of this, adjusting ingredients for these recipes is especially important. First, increase the sugar by 1 to 2 tablespoons per cup of sugar to compensate for less liquid evaporation at lower altitudes. Next, reduce each teaspoon of baking powder by $\frac{1}{8}$ of a teaspoon. Finally, reduce each cup of liquid by 2 tablespoons.

For custards: This applies to the Grand Marnier Crème Brulee. Since the boiling point at sea level is higher, this baked custard will likely set quicker at lower altitudes than in the mountains. Adjust baking time to 25 minutes or until the custard no longer jiggles.

For quick breads: This applies to the Maple Cornbread, Orange Blossom Brownies, Lemon Pound Cake, Sour Cream Coffee Cake. Increase the sugar by 1 to 2 tablespoons per cup of sugar to compensate for less liquid evaporation at lower altitudes.

For cheesecakes and pies: This applies to the Huckleberry Swirl Cheesecake, New York Cheesecake, Flathead Cherry Pie, Blueberry Cobbler, and both quiches. Expect that cheese cake and pie baked at an altitude lower than 3,000 feet will take 10 to 15 minutes less time to cook than suggested in these recipes.

Index

in Orange Blossom Brownies, 86
Walnut-Gorgonzola Salad, 35
Warren Wing, xiii
watercress in Lobster Salad, 94
Wellington, Beef, 68–69
Western Barbecue, 104–7
whipping cream. *See* heavy whipping cream
white wine
in Classic Escargot, 30
in Hollandaise Sauce, 113
in Mushroom Pepper Sauté, 21
in Seafood Bisque, 42
in Shrimp Chesapeake, 61
in Sole En Croute with Fresh Citrus Vinaigrette, 64–65
in Sundried Tomato Compound Butter, 114
in Wild Mushroom Bisque, 46
Wilcoxsons ice cream
in Flaming Orange, 87–89
in Montana Mud Pie, 79

Wild Mushroom Bisque, 46–47
Wilson, Doug, x
wine. *See also* Madeira wine; red wine; sherry; white wine
list of Chico Hot Springs Resort, 103
Port Wine Butter Sauce, 113
Port Wine Sauce, 113
Wine Cellar Dinner, 98–103
Wine Spectator, 103

Y

yellow bell peppers. *See* bell peppers (yellow)
Yellowstone Chicken, 60
Yellowstone River, 97

Z

Zenato Amarone, 99
zucchini in Vegetable Tower, 53